Soccer iQ Presents...
POSSESSION

Teaching Your Team to Keep the Darn Ball

BY DAN BLANK

ISBN: 098969772X
ISBN 13: 9780989697729

Welcome to POSSESSION, a part of the *Soccer iQ* book series.

If you would like to purchase copies of this book at a bulk discount, please email me at coach@soccerpoet.com

I invite you to read my blog and take the *Soccer iQ* quiz at www.soccerpoet.com.

I hope you'll be my Twitter friend: @SoccerPoet

For Izzy

TABLE OF CONTENTS

INTRODUCTION

I want to be perfectly clear that I am not trying to sell you on a specific style of soccer. As the coach, it's up to you to determine your team's system and style, and those things need to be predicated on your personnel. If your players aren't technically competent, a possession-based style probably won't help you win games. In other words, you can't make chicken salad out of chicken poop.

Successful possession is all about the details. It's not merely about one player passing the ball to another. It's about all of the little things that give each player the very best chance to successfully receive and pass the ball.

You bought this book to help you teach your players how to keep the ball. That's exactly what you'll get. I'll give you the building blocks for teaching your players how to connect passes. I'll provide you with a progression of exercises and the coaching points to accompany them. This book is heavy on diagrams. The diagrams are simple and should be easy to follow.

Even if you prefer to play an uber-direct style of soccer, every now and then your players are actually going to have to pass the ball to their teammates, and these exercises will help them get better at it.

This book is an if/then proposition. I'm not telling you that possession soccer is the best style for your team. All I'm saying is that *if* you want your team to play a possession style, *then* these are the things you need to do.

None of these exercises are what I would consider groundbreaking and I didn't invent any of them. But, over the past couple of decades of trying to teach my teams how to keep the ball, these are the ones I've found to be the most effective. In other words, these exercises are my favorites.

If you've read the *Soccer iQ* books, some of the coaching points will sound familiar. Some of the chapters from the *Soccer iQ* books have been pulled word for word into this text. The material is no less relevant and I couldn't exactly produce a book on possession without including those chapters. Let me put in another way: If I didn't include them, this book would be hopelessly incomplete.

This book is not about penetrating passes or scoring goals. It's about the art of keeping the ball. It's all about possession. I hope it serves you well.

SECTION 1
THE COACHING
POINTS

1

Why Possession?

I am a possession coach. You don't have to be, but I am. I played on a college team that emphasized possession and executed it well. And I liked it. Not only did I like it, I got to see firsthand the real value of keeping the ball. I got to see what it did to the guy I was marking. I got to see what it did to his teammates. On many occasions I was an eyewitness to the physical and emotional unraveling of an opponent who had spent too much of his afternoon chasing a ball he could never quite catch up to. And I liked that more than anything. So I'm a believer.

Soccer fans rally around a team that can pass the ball. It makes sense. There is something intrinsically beautiful about a long run of passes culminating with a three-man combo to an overlapping outside back who puts her serve on the head of a teammate darting in at the near post. It's soccer's answer to the 6-4-3 double play or an alley-oop. But if you think that the value of possession is more form than function, you may be missing the boat. Because every time you pass the ball, regardless of the direction your pass goes, you are making progress. The problem is that your players might not realize it.

The legendary coach, Graham Ramsay, taught me to think of each pass as a jab in a heavyweight fight. In the first few rounds those jabs have no significant effect. The boxers hardly seem to notice them. But each one of those jabs is making a dent, and in the final three rounds, those jabs start to feel like cannonballs. You see, it's not about the effectiveness of a single punch; it's about the damage done by the accumulation of those punches. The same applies for passes in a game of soccer.

A lot of coaches mix possession drills into their training sessions on a daily basis. And as long as their team is matched up against an inferior opponent, the players can showcase their ability to keep the ball. But when an evenly matched opponent makes it difficult to possess the ball, the players will panic. They will cave to the pressure, quickly abandon their style and end up looking like any other team.

Possession is a long-term investment and the market isn't always going to be kind to you. You'll have to weather some rough patches. The other team will take the ball from you. That's how soccer works. But if you are a possession team that refuses to abandon its style, you'll see your investment start to grow and then snowball.

I'll give you an example from a game my team played a few years back. In the first ten minutes we were under siege and struggled to cross midfield. Our opponent was smothering our short passes and at first we were barely able to string four passes together. But we are a possession team and we believe in the long haul. So when we couldn't string four passes together, we strung three. And if we couldn't string three, we strung two. But we kept passing the ball. And even those brief runs of possession, if you can accumulate enough of them, will have an effect. Before you knew it, our four-pass runs were becoming five, six, and seven-pass runs. The more we passed the ball, the easier it became to pass the ball. The easier it became to pass the ball, the more we passed it. The more we passed, the more they chased. As the half wore on, they began chasing with less conviction. With two minutes left in the first half we strung together

22 consecutive passes without our opponent ever touching the b
ment concluded with the three-man combo I mentioned above
whipping a cross into the head of our forward.

We didn't score on that play, but that run of 22 passes was, for all intents
and purposes, a knockout blow. Our opponent was shattered. They had done
too much chasing and were out of gas. In the second half they barely touched
the ball. We had the run of the park and scored with seven minutes left to win
1-0. That goal was the byproduct of all the passing that led up to it. Jab, jab,
jab.

Every time you pass the ball, your opponent is going to chase it. It's one
thing to chase a twenty-yard pass once or twice, but imagine having to chase
that same pass 15-20 times in a single half – at a sprint. It's tiring. It's demoral-
izing. It makes for a fatigued and frustrated opponent. And when an opponent
is tired and frustrated, that opponent will make mistakes. Players lose their
patience and start taking gambles that pull apart their team's defensive shape.
Teammates have to compensate for those gambles but they're too tired to do so
effectively. Their bodies fail them. Seams open up and chances to score practi-
cally create themselves. But you and your players have to commit to the long
haul.

Some coaches think that possession soccer is bunk. They'll tell you the
most effective way to win a game is with a direct style that gets the ball from
Point A to Point B as quickly as possible. I'm not going to argue that. There are
plenty of teams who do very well playing direct soccer, and if they're winning,
who am I to argue? Still, I prefer to cast my lot with a team that wants to keep
the ball.

There are two parts to a soccer game – the part where your team has the
ball and the part where their team has the ball. It is my belief that when you can
elongate the former and reduce the latter, you have a better chance of winning
the game. Simple, right?

2

All Aboard

If you're going to have a possession team, every player needs to buy into it. This isn't as easy as it sounds. Possession soccer requires patience. It involves making a lot of low-risk passes, and that means the ball is frequently going to move sideways and backwards. The problem is that a lot of players are programmed to go forward at all costs. They want to affect the scoreboard as quickly and as often as possible. They don't want to jab, jab, jab. They want to throw the knockout punch every time they have the ball. They aren't wired for patience, and that leads to a lot of high-risk passes which lead to a lot of turnovers.

If you're going to be a possession team, then you need a team full of players who are committed to possessing the ball. All it takes is one impatient player to undo all the good work your team has been doing. To combat this, you have to sell your style. The players need to know what they're doing and *why* they're doing it. That's where your sales pitch matters. In the previous chapter I detailed the value of possession. It's up to you to beat your players over the head with that information morning, noon and night.

Remember, making the opponent chase is a long-term investment. Your players need to understand the long-term effects of being patient. Possession soccer is more than *we have the ball and you don't*. It's about how we grind you down *because* we have the ball and you don't. It's about all the physical and emotional energy you'll burn trying to get the ball back, and how that will eventually come back to haunt you.

To establish a possession style in your team, you've got to hammer home the point of keeping the ball. Until every player understands that *you* don't have to win the game every time *you* touch the ball, a possession style will never take root. When it comes to possession soccer, one bad apple will spoil your bunch.

3

Numbers

As you teach your players how to keep the ball, you need to teach them to count. Your players don't have to be world-class mathematicians, but they all need the ability to look at a snapshot of the field and immediately identify good numbers or bad numbers. Good numbers means that your team has a numerical advantage. Bad numbers means the opponent has you outnumbered.

Obviously you are a lot more likely to keep the ball when you have good numbers and a lot less likely to keep it when the numbers are bad. But because soccer is such a fluid game, the numbers are constantly in flux, and because the ball is a magnet for the opponent, good numbers will quickly become bad ones. This the very reason why we coach our teams to switch the field of play, right? *It's too crowded down the right side, so let's try the left.*

A player who is about to receive the ball needs to understand what the numerical situation is in her area of the field. Now, when the numbers around her are good, she's likely going to pass the ball to a teammate in her immediate vicinity. No problem there. The problems occur when the player receiving the ball is in an area of bad numbers. Just because the numbers are bad, that doesn't necessarily mean that she won't have a short passing option; many times she will. And when she plays that short option, that's typically when the area gets too crowded and the ball is lost. As coaches, we need to recognize that in this situation, it wasn't the second player who is necessarily at fault for losing the ball; it may have been the fault of the first player who put her teammate in an unwinnable situation.

The key is for the player receiving the ball to know that the numbers around her are turning bad before the ball is ever at her feet, and then finding the pass that gets the ball to an area where the numbers are more favorable. Often times that pass is going to have to cover 25 yards or more and it may have to be in the air.

Keeping the ball involves a constant search for good numbers. After two or three short passes, chances are the numbers are going to start turning bad. When the numbers start turning bad, it's time to look for a bigger ball that is going to relieve pressure. That's one way possession undoes the opponent: you suck them in with a few short passes and then eliminate them with a bigger one, and then the process starts over in another area of the field.

Coaches often run possession exercises in small areas. The danger of this is that players become conditioned to look for short passes and their vision starts to max out at 15 or 20 yards, and they shy away from playing a ball in the air. It is critical to mix in possession exercises that require a big space, because often times it takes a bigger pass to turn bad numbers into good numbers.

When you are running possession exercises, make sure your players are constantly evaluating the numbers. Make sure they understand when they can play short and when they need to play the bigger ball. Teach your players to count.

4

Spacing

A good bit of coaching is leading our players to their *Aha!* moments. When it comes to spacing, you'll have to flip the switch a whole bunch of times before the bulb actually lights. And you're going to have to light one bulb at a time, many times over.

When the opponent has the ball, you want to make the field small; you want to make the opponent play in a crowded field. By that same token, when your team has the ball, you want to make the field big. You want to make the opponent cover large expanses of land to pressure the ball. Think of it like an egg on a table. When the opponent has the ball, you want the field to look like that egg – nice and tight and compact. Now, smash that egg on the table and see how much more area it covers. That's what you want it to look like when your team has the ball.

When it comes to possession, every inch matters, and I mean that literally. If you can make it so an opponent has to cover ten feet to tackle the ball, don't settle for nine feet and eleven inches. This is one of the most prominent mistakes players will make during possession exercises. Instead of standing on the boundary line (or even a half-step wide of it), they'll stand a step or two inside of it. Unacceptable. Every inch of space you waste is an inch you are conceding to the opponent. Every wasted inch is one less inch of work the opponent has to do to get the ball back. Smart possession players are greedy about that inch because they know that the further the opponent has to chase to get the ball, the less likely she is to actually get it.

Spacing also means keeping the field balanced with your numbers. As I mentioned earlier, the ball is like a magnet, but not just for the opponent. Think of all the players as if they were marbles on a table. Wherever the ball is, the table tilts in that direction and all the marbles start rolling that way. When your own marbles start rolling toward the ball, that's when the field starts shrinking. The inches you're conceding soon become feet and the feet become yards and any way you slice it, your players are doing some of the opponents' job for them and before you know it, you're trying to keep the ball in a very crowded patch of land.

When the field gets crowded, you need an exit strategy to move the ball to a less congested area. That requires discipline from some players to keep their distance from the ball or even move further away from it. Remember, we suck the opponents toward the ball, then we play past them. To do that, we need players who won't get hypnotized and start zombie-walking toward the ball. Your players have to understand the value of keeping the field big when your team has the ball, otherwise they'll just zombie on over and shrink the field.

When teaching possession, demand discipline in spacing. This is a lot easier when your players understand why it's important, so keep hitting them over the head with its significance.

5

Speed of Play

In *Soccer iQ* I referred to speed of play as soccer's Holy Grail because speed of play is what wins games. It is particularly important for a team that wants to play possession soccer. If you are a possession team and your speed of play is slow, you're going to lose a lot of games.

If your team is going to be effective at keeping the ball, then speed of play has to become a major priority. The faster you play, the more difficult it is for the opponent to get organized defensively. The faster you play, the more difficult it becomes for the opponent to dispossess you. In short, the faster you play, the better off you are.

Speed of play is another area where, as a coach, you have to sell, sell, sell! Remember, you're probably dealing with players who are pre-programmed to throw the knockout punch. Those players tend to take longer on the ball as they consider all the magnificent ways they will win the game. Until players understand and internalize the value of speed of play, they'll never play as fast as you want them to play.

I'll give you an example that you're probably familiar with. You run a possession exercise with a one or two-touch restriction and man, things are really humming! Your team looks fantastic! Then you move into a scrimmage, and as soon as you put goals on the field, it looks like your team is playing underwater. Suddenly everyone is taking four or five touches and hemming and hawing every time the ball is at their feet. Your team's speed of play has died a mysterious death and you're left scratching your head. Sound familiar?

It is my categorical belief that to play fast, *you have to want to play fast*. If there's a noticeable decrease in your team's speed of play once you eliminate the touch restrictions, it's because your players have not internalized the intrinsic value of speed of play. To play fast, your players have to *want to play fast*, and they won't want to play fast until they fully comprehend why it's important. It's easy to stop a two-touch possession exercise when a player takes three touches, but what do you do when there are no touch restrictions? What do you do when a player takes two touches when she could've got the job done with one?

One of my coaching mantras is this: *If you can get it done with one touch, don't take two. If you can get it done with two, don't take three.* I will stop any exercise at any point if a player is taking more touches than necessary. My point is that you can't just coach speed of play through touch restrictions. You need to coach it and sell it all the time. You need your players to internalize the value of playing fast if they are ever going to be successful at keeping the ball.

Incidentally, an oft-overlooked component of speed of play is simply the speed that the ball moves from one player to the next. Too many American players just don't kick the ball hard enough when they are passing to a teammate's feet. We under-hit our passes when we need to over-hit them. If you want a comparison, watch any EPL match. Take a look at how hard the players smack the ball into their teammates when they are playing a 20-yard ball into feet. That sucker is humming! Too many of our players try to kiss the ball to their teammates and that's just too darn slow.

If your objective is to become a team that's good in possession, then you have to get the ball moving faster than an opponent can run – much faster! In all of your technical exercises, demand that your players put enough zip on their passes. If you play a pass along the ground into your teammate's foot, she needs to be able to control it, I don't care how fast that ball is moving!

6

KISS

Keep it simple, Silly.

As coaches we are always trying to simplify the game for our players. We are always looking for ways to make them successful by doing less. This is the war of wills we wage against our players when it comes to possession soccer.

As far as pure possession exercises go, all a player can really do to be successful is connect a pass. Now there are degrees to that success, but the bottom line is that in an exercise that is strictly possession-themed, there is no incentive for dribbling past an opponent and there are no goals to shoot at. The very best a player can do is pass the ball to a teammate. And yet we still have players who get themselves into all types of trouble because they refuse to take the simple solution. Imagine how much more difficult those players become when there are actually goals on the field!

To be successful at keeping the ball, your players have to be willing to do the simple things and do them quickly. They need to remember all those reasons why your team is trying to keep the ball and they need to understand that there's no harm in connecting a five-yard pass even if it doesn't put the ball directly in front of the opponent's goal.

Possession soccer means a lot of low-risk passes. That's what KISS means. It means taking the safer alternative. It means saying no to the homerun ball unless there's a darn good chance of it being successful. It means 11 players making it as difficult as possible for the opponent to win back the ball. A lot of time that means choosing a very pedestrian passing option instead of the ball for glory.

I once coached a midfielder who was wholly unremarkable as an attacking presence, but she was extremely reliable when it came to keeping the ball for our team. She always played with one or two touches and always connected her passes. During a team meeting I was using her as an example of someone who did a fantastic job of playing quick and simple soccer. This is what she said: *"The way I see it, the more touches I take, the more likely I am to lose the ball, so I just try to get it to a teammate as soon as possible."*

That wasn't just great, it was freaking profound! This player knew she wasn't a star. She knew she was technically and athletically limited. But she had figured out that if she just kept passing the ball to our team, she'd stay on the field, so she chose to play the simplest possible soccer.

Every now and then you need your special players to do something special to break pressure on their own, but for the most part, anyone can play simply if they just *choose* to do it. Your battle as a coach is convincing your players that it's okay to choose the simplest path. There's nothing wrong with connecting a simple pass even if it does nothing more than keep possession. All those simple passes are the jabs that wear down your opponent.

Possession soccer often breaks down when a player tries to do too much. You've got to rewire your knockout punchers. You've got to turn them into boxers. You've got to reprogram them to internalize the big picture so they see the inherent value of keeping the ball.

7

What's Next?

To keep it simple, your players have to play fast. To play fast, they have to know what's next.

One of the main culprits behind a loss of possession is slow play, and a major cause of slow play is players who don't make their decisions until after the ball has arrived at their feet. Because soccer is such a fluid game, the picture is always changing. Passing seams appear, disappear and reappear. Good numbers quickly become bad numbers. All the pieces are in a constant state of flux, so what was a good idea a half-second ago might now be an awful idea.

It is very common for a player to receive the ball, focus on controlling it, and then pick her head up and begin the decision-making process. And that's a big problem. Every second it takes her to make a decision is another second that the opponent has to adjust, organize defensively, close ground and pressure the ball.

It is impossible for a player to play quickly if she has to make her decisions after she has the ball. For your players to keep the ball, they need to know what options are available to them before the ball gets to their feet. In short, they have to know what's next. And that's a question they should never stop asking.

The real value of one-touch exercises is that they force players to make decisions before they receive the ball. To make these decisions they have to constantly be taking film of the field and figuring out what they're going to do if the ball finds them. One-touch exercises force players to ask, *"What's next?"*

Incidentally, this is a question they need to be asking even when the other team has the ball. When the opposing team has the ball, a smart player is formulating a plan *just in case* the ball finds her.

Early in my coaching career, if I was running a one-touch exercise, I would allow a player from the defending team an extra touch if she intercepted a pass. It seemed a lot to ask of a player to make a defensive play and an attacking one all with a single touch. Eventually I got rid of that bonus-touch clause because I wanted the players to think about their attacking options even as they defended, the same way I want players considering their defensive responsibilities even as we attack. Eliminating the bonus touch made the possession exercises sloppier, but I think it's a good trade. It's more important for my players to ask *What's next? What if the ball comes to me?* than it is for the exercise to run without a hiccup. If you're running one-touch exercises, this is an important coaching point.

Not every exercise you do is going to have a one-touch restriction, and there certainly won't be a one-touch restriction on match day, so you have to get your players to internalize the question. When the game is being played, you want all of your players asking, "What's next?" The only way I know to do that is to hit them over the head with the question as often as possible, so that's what I do. I bombard them with it whenever possible because I know that if they don't know what's next before the ball is at their feet, our speed of play is going to suffer and that is going to hinder our ability to keep the ball.

To keep the ball, speed of play has to be a priority. That can only happen when your players know what's next.

Play the Way
You Face

A huge percentage of turnovers are the result of a player trying to receive the ball from one direction and then turn and play it in the opposite direction, particularly if she is trying to advance the ball up the field. Half the time the player receiving the ball turns directly into a pressuring opponent and loses the ball. Other times the player is too off-balance to technically execute the pass, or the pass is too predictable, or the pass is just too darn difficult to be successful. In *Soccer iQ* I referred to this as the *Impossible Pass*. Any way you slice it, the ball now belongs to the other team.

When it comes to keeping things simple, this is one where a lot of players lose the plot because they don't understand risk management. There is no easier way to pass the ball than the way you are facing. You can see any obstacles in your way and you can usually execute with a single touch. It doesn't get much simpler than that.

That simple negative pass also gets the ball to a teammate who is facing forward, and that's the direction you ultimately want to go. So what the player who receives the initial pass can't see, the player to whom she drops the ball can. In essence, you're investing a ball back for a ball forward. Remember that: *A ball back for a ball forward.* Players need to understand that the negative pass is an investment in the forward one that follows it. Often, this two-player combination actually gets the ball forward more quickly than a single player trying to do it on her own.

When you are coaching your possession exercises, look for those moments when a player who could've played the way she was facing loses the ball because she chose a more difficult path. Then, freeze the moment and restart the action from the player who passed her the ball and have the guilty party make a better choice.

Again, the reason a lot of players won't choose to play the way they face is that there is no glory in a negative ball. A ball back for a ball forward is a cornerstone of possession soccer and your players need to embrace it. When a player is taking bad risks instead of playing the way she faces, she doesn't yet get it. You need 11 players on the field who get it, Coach, so sell, sell, sell!

9

Passing Angles and Empathy

S o far we've only discussed the role of the player on the ball, but possession is everyone's job. The player on the ball is going to need a lot of help from her teammates if your team is going to keep the ball. That help begins with passing angles and a healthy dose of empathy.

A passing angle is a seam that runs between players (usually opponents), or between players and boundaries, that the ball can travel through without being intercepted or deflected. When a player receives the ball, there is always a seam (unless she is completely surrounded). A teammate who wants the ball must work to receive the ball in one of these seams. Because soccer is a fluid game, these seams are constantly moving - appearing, disappearing and reappearing. A smart player can read the flow of bodies between her and the ball to identify the seams that give the ball-carrier the best chance of passing her the ball and she will *work* to get into one of those seams.

As I mentioned earlier, when it comes to possession, nothing ranks higher than speed of play. The ability to move the ball faster than the opposition can run and organize itself is the surest way to keep the ball and carve up the opponent. Moving the ball quickly depends on the player receiving the ball to make quick decisions. That player's ability to make quick decisions depends on the options available to her as the ball arrives. Those options are entirely predicated upon her teammates' ability to quickly identify and move into passing seams.

We frequently want our players to play with one touch. A player cannot do that if she doesn't have teammates giving her useful options, particularly in the direction she is facing. But if at least one teammate can get into a useful seam in that direction, the player can receive and pass the ball in a single touch — and there is no faster speed of play than one-touch passing.

Sounds simple, right? Well in theory it is. But watch any possession exercise and you'll see countless examples of players who get anchored in dead space instead of working to get into a seam. And because of that you'll see countless examples of a team losing the ball when it absolutely didn't have to lose it.

Identifying a seam should be easy. It takes one solitary quality — *empathy*. Players need to empathize with the teammate who is about to receive the ball. They need to ask themselves, "If I was her, and I wanted to play with one touch, where would I want my teammate to be?" Well, they wouldn't want her hiding behind opponents. They'd want her in a seam that ran between opponents. Identifying that seam is Step 1.

Step 2 is actually moving their feet to get into that seam. The only question they need to ask themselves now is whether or not they actually want the ball, because they're not going to get it if they're hiding behind an opponent. The ball can't travel through opponents, but it can sure as heck travel through that seam. To get the ball, make a teammate's life easy and get into that seam.

Another problem you'll encounter when a supporting player gives a bad passing angle is that the player on the ball will momentarily suspend rational thought and try to pass the ball to that teammate anyway. Of course the ball won't get there. Make sure your players know that until the ball arrives at the target, it is the passer's responsibility. In other words, don't pass a ball to a teammate who has given an unacceptable passing angle. Either pass it to the proper angle and let the teammate go get it (assuming it is safe to do so) or find another option. But don't pretend that a bad passing angle is going to work.

Passing angles are absolutely critical to your team's ability to keep the ball. Don't be afraid to stop your possession exercises every single time a player gives a passing angle that is less than perfect. You've got to be willing to hammer away at this point day after day after day. Just because a player understands where to go, it doesn't automatically mean that she'll go there. You've got to drive this point home every chance you get.

10

Receiving with the Proper Foot

Once a supporting player has identified and moved into the proper seam, the next part is making that tiny, little extra effort to make sure the ball comes to her proper foot, which is normally going to be the foot furthest from the opponent who will be pressuring the pass she's about to receive.

For your team to keep the ball, merely getting into the proper seam isn't enough. Players must also understand which foot needs to be the one receiving the ball. They need to have decisions made before the ball gets to them and those decisions will dictate which foot should be the one receiving the ball. When deciding which foot to receive the ball with, a player must ask herself these questions:

Which foot will help me escape pressure?
Which foot will help me advance the ball?
Which foot will set up my next pass?

And by all means, don't let a player take that first touch into pressure. She needs to be prepared to receive the ball and immediately put her body between the ball and the pressuring opponent.

Regardless of which foot receives the ball, players need to remember that they don't always get to take two touches. There's no rule that says you're entitled to settle every ball that comes to you. Your players need to be prepared to play with a single touch because often times, that's all they're going to get. If they don't have the necessary time and space to settle the ball, they can't pretend that they do. Hound them to make the adjustment and play with one-touch. The ability to make these small adjustments can literally mean the margin of victory to your team.

Players who receive the ball with the wrong foot either don't know what they're doing wrong or they're being lazy. The only way to make this a habit is to demand perfection during training sessions. Details matter.

11

Receiving Across
the Standing Leg

A player's ability to receive a ball across her standing leg is a critical little
thing when it comes to keeping the ball as a team. It is an essential building
block to the whole concept of passing and receiving.

Receiving across my standing leg means that if a pass is arriving from my
left side, I'm going to let the ball roll across the front of my body, open up my
hips and receive it with the inside of my right foot. This allows me to open up
my body which in turn opens up more of the field for me. If I receive that pass
with my left foot or I don't open up my body when receiving it with my right,
I'll end up receiving it with my hips squared up to the teammate who passed
me the ball. This not only reduces my passing options, but it puts me under
undo pressure if an opponent is chasing that pass, and that's a pretty common
occurrence.

Opening up my hips and letting that ball roll across my standing leg allows the ball to run for extra yard or so, and that's another yard that a chasing opponent has to cover. Plus it puts me in a position to immediately get my body between the ball and the opponent who is chasing it.

This isn't the world's most difficult skill, but it gets a lot more difficult when a player is running one direction and then has to do a quick pirouette, backpedal, then open up to receive the ball. *The Letter L* is a technical exercise to help improve this skill.

The Letter L – Exercise for Receiving across the Standing Leg

The timing of the pass is critical in this exercise, so it'll probably take a few repetitions before the players get the hang of it. The player receiving the ball should be travelling at something close to full speed just before she adjusts to open up her hips.

The server plays a crisp, ten-yard pass into the empty space. I set a cone behind the area just as a target for the direction of that pass. It's important that the server's pass is directly straight and not angled back into the worker's run. The worker sprints to get on the end of the serve. She opens up her hips, receives it with her right foot, then quickly dribbles back to her starting spot. In the next round, the worker's second touch is a pass to the next person in line.

Variations
- Instead of passing with the inside of the foot, pass with a toe poke.
- The worker must not let her right foot touch the ground between receiving the ball and passing it.
- The worker plays her pass with just one touch.
- The worker opens up, fakes the dribble back to her starting spot, then spins out and dribbles the opposite direction.

The Letter 'L' Exercise

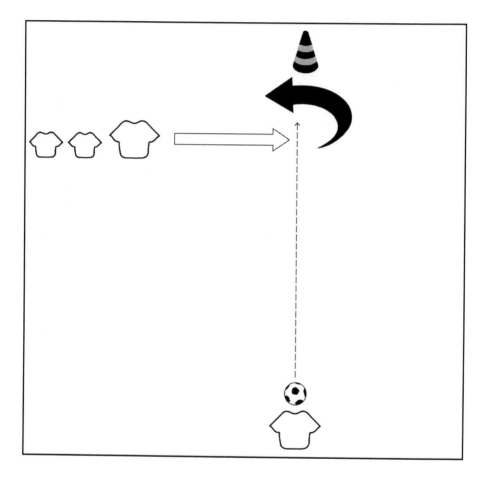

12

Playing to the Proper Foot

Players must always remember the value of speed of play. A player has to set up her teammate so that she can play quickly or at the very least have a fighting chance of keeping possession of the ball. And that means passing the ball to her proper foot.

Soccer is full of little big things and this is one of them. It's astonishing how many potentially great attacks are not stymied by the opponent but rather by one of our own players passing the ball to the wrong foot.

The player on the ball has to empathize with the teammate who will receive it and has to give her the best chance to be successful. Sometimes it's so obvious that it's literally painful. If she passes the ball to a teammate's left foot, that teammate can protect it from the opponent who is closing her down. But if she plays it to her right foot, it becomes a 50-50 ball and the teammate gets clobbered by a thundering tackle.

Here's an example from a training session with a player I'll call Jackie Jones. We were playing 5v5+GKs and Jackie received the ball, back to goal at the penalty spot. Jackie had heavy pressure on her so she decided to lay the ball back to her wide-open teammate, Meghan. Meghan hit a first-time shot from 22 yards that she shanked wide. At that point I stopped training and this conversation followed:

DB: Jackie, how long have you known Meghan?
JJ: 3 Years.
DB: And can you tell me what her strong foot is?
JJ: Her left.
DB: So why did you pass the ball to her right foot?
JJ: Because I'm an idiot.

Okay, Jackie is by no means an idiot, but her pass was in fact idiotic. Meghan is one of the best strikers of the ball I've ever seen... *with her left foot.* Jackie knew that, but didn't put enough thought into her pass for it to do her team any good. At our level this is an unacceptable mental error.

To keep the ball at a high level, players must to hold themselves to a higher standard. Merely getting the ball to a teammate is no longer good enough. They've got to put that teammate in the best possible position and that means delivering the proper ball to her proper foot. Here's a really simple way to sell it: *Give a pass that you'd like to receive.* Don't bounce it into your teammate if you can just as easily keep the ball on the ground. Don't smash it at her abdomen when you can pass it to her feet. And don't pass it to her right foot if she needs it on her left.

Hound your players about passing to the proper foot because it is an essential detail to keeping the ball. If a player passes to the wrong foot in a possession game, let her know about it. In possession exercises, make a rule that passing the ball to the wrong foot is an automatic forfeiture of possession. You've got to mind the details if you expect your team to keep the ball.

13

Passing Angles, Proper Feet and Hockey Sticks

I've come to believe that if you don't spell it out for your players, plenty of them are going to miss whatever point you are trying to make. When it comes to passing angles and offering the proper foot, here's how I introduce it to the players. This is an extremely dull and static demonstration, and it's going to sound even duller in print, but it makes the point very well.

When an opponent gets into your passing seam, imagine that player has a hockey stick. The area on either side of her body that she can cover with that stick is her space. The ball won't make it through her space. Therefore, you have to provide an angle that is wide of that hockey stick's reach.

You'll demonstrate this with the help of two players, one who will be the passer and one who will be the defender. Position them ten yards apart. You'll also need some cones, plus two street-hockey sticks or brooms or mops... anything with a long handle will do. Give those two hockey sticks to the defender. As you explain this exercise, start with the inactive players observing from the end of the area nearest the ball. Then you'll need them to move to the end opposite of the ball. It's important that the players are observing from the ends of the area and not the sides of it.

Establish the reach of the hockey sticks on either side of the defender. Make sure the defender stands upright. Have her start with the hockey stick along her right leg, then slide it out to the side. When she can no longer slide the stick along the ground without leaning, mark that spot with a cone. Then do the same thing on her other side. At this point your defender should look something like the Eifel Tower, with the hockey sticks representing the reach of her legs if she stuck out a foot to intercept a pass.

Now, run a line of cones from the blades of the hockey sticks to the ball to form a 'V'. Everything inside the V is the defender's space. For a pass to be successful, the ball has to travel wide of the V. Simple, yes?

Now, pick up all those cones and tell the players to replace them with an imaginary line. It's time to have the defender pull in those sticks and time to move all the observing players to the opposite end.

The first objective of this exercise is for the players to be able to tell you when you've given the passer an acceptable passing angle. So you are going to start in dead space, directly behind the defender. Taking one sideways step at a time, ask the observing players if you are giving an acceptable angle. Ask them after each step you take. When you get close to an acceptable angle, some players will take the bait. When one does, have the defender reach out that hockey stick. If it breaks the line between your feet and the ball, the passing angle is unacceptable. And even if it doesn't quite break that line, you may still have the chance to make an important point.

Remember, we said it's no longer good enough to merely get the ball to a teammate; now we need to get it to the proper foot. The proper foot is going to be the forward foot – the one furthest from the ball. For the passer to get the ball to the proper foot, that forward foot also needs to get wide of that imaginary line. This is one of your big coaching moments in this demonstration, so don't miss it! When you make the adjustment to receive the ball with the forward foot, that hockey stick might just break the line.

Ask all the players if they understand it. They'll say they do because they'll be bored and want to move onto other things. Now, have half of them form a line as the passer while the other half forms a line to take your spot as the supporting player. Have the supporting player quickly pop out of dead space and stop immediately when she's given an acceptable passing angle. When that player freezes, ask the passer if the angle is acceptable. Then have the defender hold out the hockey stick to see if they got it right. If they did, have the passer play the ball into the supporting player's forward foot. Then it's time for the next two players to go. Have the players switch lines after their turn. I have the players take only one turn in each role because like I said, this isn't the most exciting thing they'll ever do.

Incidentally, the hockey sticks give a little too much credit to the defender's reach. That's not by accident. I'll take an angle that is slightly bigger than necessary over an angle that isn't quite big enough. There's no harm in providing a little cushion with your passing angles.

In this diagram, we have an imaginary (dashed) line representing the defender's space. You start in dead space directly behind the defender and methodically work your way to a better angle.

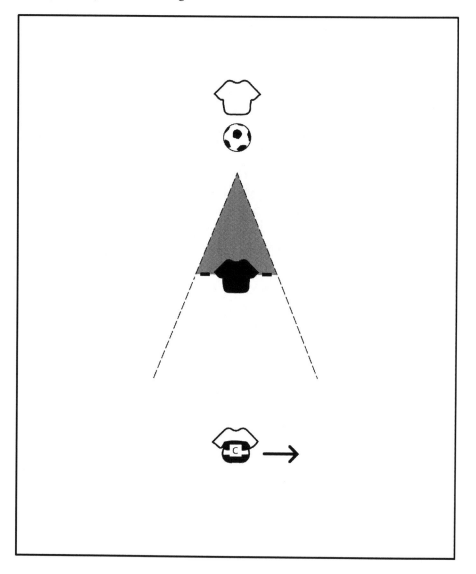

In this diagram, you have moved to an acceptable angle of support, wide of the imaginary line.

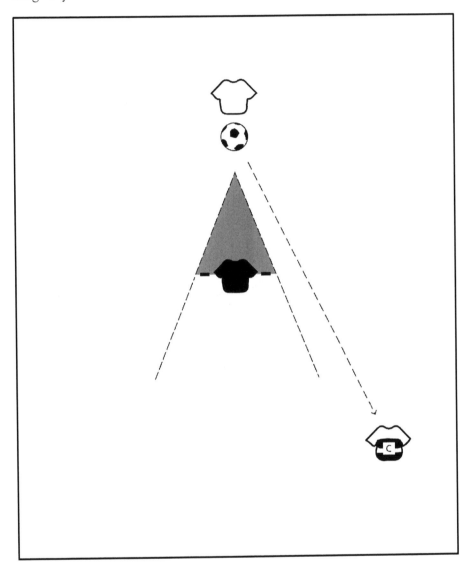

14

Better Than Square

We have already discussed playing the way you face, but a player can't do that if her teammates aren't taking up proper supporting positions. For a player to play the way she's facing, she needs support underneath her. The supporting teammate must choose an angle of support that makes the target's life as easy as possible for a one-touch layoff.

Too often the supporting player runs past the target player as the ball arrives at the target's feet. When she runs past the target player, there is no easy way (and often times no way at all) for the target to deliver her the ball with a single touch. Common sense says that the ball can't magically pass through the defender's body, so barring some type of miraculous flick-on, the supporting teammate has run herself out of any useful position.

To provide a useful angle of support, supporting players can't run past the player on the ball. They have got to give her the opportunity to play the way she's facing. And just because they haven't run completely past her, it doesn't necessarily mean they've given her a good angle. When the angle of support they give her requires a perfectly square lay-off, they haven't made her life much easier.

Often times, when the ball arrives at the target's feet, the supporting player has gone so high up the field that only a square pass - an absolutely flawless square pass lay-off – will do the trick. This is better than running past the target, but only slightly. The target can play the way she's facing, but just barely, and she has no margin for error whatsoever. She has to play a perfect ball that keeps her teammate perfectly in stride and that's an awful lot of perfection to ask of anyone. If the timing of her layoff is skewed by even one millisecond, the supporting teammate will overrun her pass. And once she's overrun it, she's not going to be able to stop, turn around and retrieve it. That play has died and the opponent has taken the ball. Additionally, even if the target does play the perfect square pass, the pressuring defender may have an opportunity to stick a toe out and deflect it away.

The simple solution here is for the supporting player to put on the brakes and give the target a bigger angle. Instead of flying by the target and asking her to do something remarkable, the supporting player can just slow down and hold her run and support underneath so the target can play the way she is facing. That's how to give an angle of support that is better than square.

If the supporting player stops underneath the target, her layoff doesn't have to be perfect – it just has to be decent. All she has to do is lay the ball down somewhere in front of her support. The supporting player can always come forward to adjust to the pass.

The white area below the target represents the area that is better than square. As the Target receives the ball with pressure on her back, Attacker #2 has run herself out of a useful supporting angle by advancing beyond the target. Attacker #3 offers support in a useful spot underneath the target. She has made the Target's life easier by supporting better than square, allowing the Target to play the way she is facing.

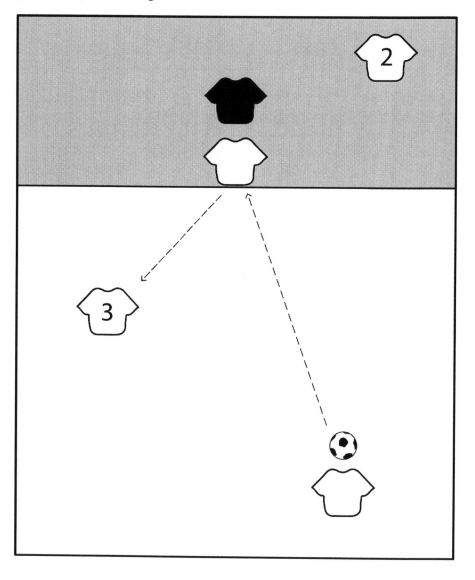

15

Playing Behind the Fence

Look at the central player in this diagram:

S he's moved between — and in front of — two opponents to offer support for the teammate on the ball. The problem is that when she receives that pass, she is in front of those two opponents and they've seen the whole play develop, so it is easy for them to quickly close her down. This will make it almost impossible for her to turn. It will make it very difficult for her to do anything other than to pass the ball back to the teammate who initially passed it to her. We can do better than that, and it's a really simple fix.

Imagine that a fence runs between those two opponents. When you receive it in front of them, you are fenced in. But if you stay behind them and behind their line of vision, the ball can get to you outside of that fence. If you receive it behind the fence, you've got an excellent chance of breaking pressure. You will be in a much better position to turn and you will have many more options once you do.

Remember, soccer has a bit of hide-and-seek in it. It's the defender's job to find the attackers. It's not the attacker's job to jump in front of them and say, *"Hey Everybody! Here I am!"* We need to be a little sneakier than that. If we can receive the ball behind the fence, our life is a lot easier.

This is a principle that all players need to understand, but it is particularly crucial for your central midfielders. They are the players who link your backs to your forwards and your left side to your right. They are the ones who often determine whether or not your team breaks pressure. They need to put themselves in the best possible position to turn the ball. When you coach possession exercises, look for these moments. Getting your central players to understand this concept will have a lot to do with how well your team keeps the ball.

In this situation, the fence is represented by the dashed line. The supporting player stays behind the fence and is in a much better position to turn when she receives the ball.

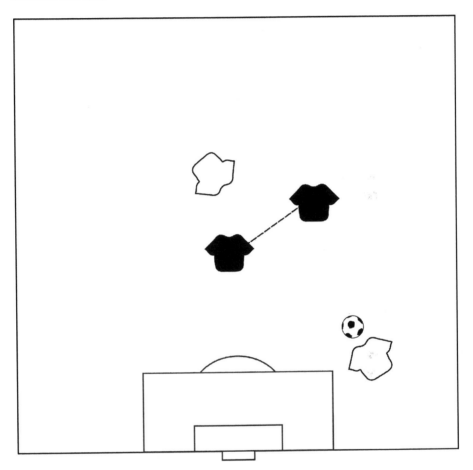

16

The Higher of
Two Options

If you are looking to play a forward pass and you can successfully deliver it to your closest teammate who is ten yards in front of you, or you can successfully deliver that pass to a teammate ten yards farther up the field, play the bigger pass. Here's why...

If you play the ball to the closest teammate and she has to play the way she is facing, you might be her only passing option. If you play a ten-yard pass to her and she plays a ten-yard pass right back to you, you've gained no ground. However, if you play the twenty yard pass and the teammate who receives it plays the way she is facing, the bypassed teammate is already underneath the target and immediately becomes an option to receive that next ball. So you play a 20-yard forward pass and your target plays a ten-yard negative pass, well then you've gained ten yards and the final player in that puzzle is facing the direction your team wants to go.

The ball is like a magnet, especially for opposing players, and they are going to gravitate toward the ball. So, beyond the simple territorial gain, the longer pass is more likely to break the opponent's pressure and the recipient of the longer pass is more likely to have a wider variety of options upon receiving the ball. These are good things.

This is a common issue for teams that play with two levels of midfielders, such as an attacking center mid and a defensive center mid. When a defender has possession of the ball, the defensive center mid is often the closest and therefore easiest option, so we tend to give her the ball. But if we can stretch our vision another fifteen yards up the field, we may find a clear path into the attacking center mid. If we can get her the ball, then the defensive center mid becomes an option for that next pass.

When it comes to instituting a pattern like the one in the diagram, the key is making sure the lower player doesn't get directly between the ball and the higher target. If she moves onto that line, she clogs the ball's path to the higher player and eliminates her as an option. At that point the lower player is, in effect, playing for the other team. If she starts to clog that seam, the higher player has to tell her to get out.

The diagram illustrates a typical situation where the longer pass eliminates more opponents and gives the target a built-in passing option underneath her.

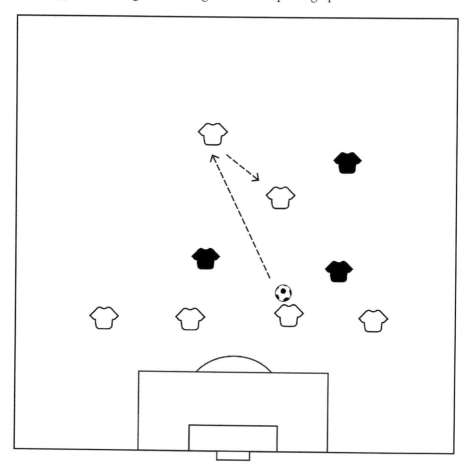

17

My Seam!

Since we closed the last chapter with the idea of two players occupying the same seam, I figured it'd be a good idea to discuss it in a little more detail. Soccer is a pretty simple game, and this is one of most advanced tactical issues that players encounter.

It is not uncommon for a player to provide a good supporting angle 20 yards away from the ball, only to have a teammate who is ten yards away from the ball wander into that same seam. A common example is when an outside back has the ball and the center forward moves into a viable passing seam. Then a central midfielder slides into that same seam, effectively cutting out her teammate who is higher up the field.

There are exceptions to what I'm about to say, but as a good rule of thumb, the player who is farther away from the ball owns the seam. Why? Because she can see a bigger picture. In the above example, the center-midfielder only sees what's between her and the outside back. She doesn't see her forward teammate behind her. The forward also sees what's between her and the outside back, and that includes the midfielder. The forward can see more pieces of the puzzle.

Now, when I say that forward owns the seam, I mean she has the right of first refusal. If she thinks the midfielder is a better option in that seam, she can move herself into a different position. But more often, the forward is going to be the better option if for no other reason than the bigger pass will eliminate more opponents and advance the ball further up the field.

This isn't just for vertical passes. It also applies to horizontal passes and even negative ones. The teammate further away from the ball almost always has the best field of vision, so it's up to her to decide who gets to occupy that seam. When that player decides that she is the best occupant of that seam, it's up to her to get the intruding teammate out of the way. How does she do that? Simple. She just demands that her teammate, "GET OUT!"

This can be a tough topic for players to get the hang of, but it's important nonetheless. The bigger pass is often the one that decisively breaks pressure. You don't want your players being their own worst enemies by clogging up perfectly good seams. If you watch advanced players, it's not uncommon to hear them telling one another to get out of a certain space. And they don't do it kindly. It's direct and loud and to the point. An advanced player knows that when a teammate tells her to get out, she should vacate that space immediately.

Here's the good news... If your team is at a point where this is the most pressing problem, then you've graduated to some seriously advanced themes of possession. Congratulations!

A passing seam runs from the right back to the left-central midfielder, but the right-central midfielder has wandered into that seam. It's up to the left-central midfielder to tell her teammate to get out of that seam.

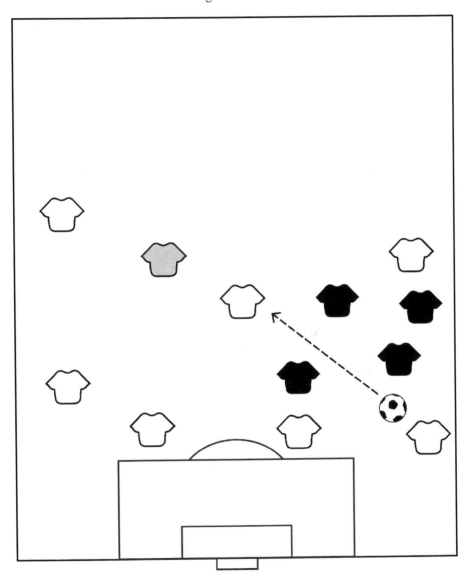

18

The Three-Step Rule

O ften times the player who has the best chance to support the player receiving the ball is the player who just passed it. That means it's extremely important for that player to quickly give a great angle of support. Players must learn to instantly transition from being the passing player to being a supporting one. That's why it's an excellent idea to teach your players the three-step rule.

The three-step rule simply means that as soon as the ball leaves her foot, the passing player must immediately take three steps in whichever direction will make it possible for her to receive a return pass.

Normally, when you make a pass, a defender is going to chase the ball. When she chases, she will move into the ball's wake, as if the ball were pulling her along by a string. Her movement into that path means that she has put herself between the passer of the ball and the person about to receive the it, and that leaves the passer in dead space. Thankfully there's an easy fix. Normally, getting out of dead space is a matter of taking three steps to either side. A player who takes these three steps quickly enough becomes a viable passing option for her teammate.

We run a lot of possession games with the three-step rule. Anytime a player passes the ball, she must immediately take at least three steps to give a better passing angle. If she doesn't, we stop the game and award possession of the ball to the opposing team.

For teams that value keeping the ball, three steps (at least) is a very valuable habit.

19

Face the Field

One of the problems a player will run into when her angle of support isn't quite good enough is that she will have to receive the pass with the wrong foot and will end up facing the sideline. This puts her at an immediate disadvantage and makes her life harder than it should be. You'll see this all the time in your possession games. Whenever possible, a player should try to receive the ball facing the biggest part of the field, because that's where she'll have the most passing options. That's one more reason why it's so important for your players to understand the difference between an acceptable passing angle and an unacceptable one, and often times it's just a matter of taking one more step. Don't let you players settle for a passing angle that's merely good enough to receive the ball when they can just as easily give an angle that will allow them to receive the ball with the proper foot *and* face the field.

By that same token, the passer of the ball has to play the proper foot when the opportunity presents itself, and you've got to hammer home that point also. But that's not exactly why I'm writing this chapter. So far everything we've talked about has been playing the ball to a teammate's feet, but sometimes we have to play it into a space where a teammate can go get it. In your possession games, these passes will often lead to a player receiving the ball facing the boundary instead of facing the field, and a lot of times it doesn't have to end up that way. In these situations, much of the responsibility rests with the passer's ability to properly weight her pass.

Many times the passer will put too much weight on her pass, and her teammate won't have time to spin around and face the field when receiving it. But if she hits that same pass with a bit less pace on it, her target can open up to the field before receiving it. This gives her the chance to evaluate her options before she's even touched the ball.

You'll commonly encounter this scenario during a possession exercise when the players have all crowded into one half of the grid, then one team wins the ball and tries to break out and exploit the empty space at the other end. The player on the ball will lead her teammate with a pass into that space, but because the pass is so heavy, the target will have to scurry just to keep the ball in bounds. Often times it ends up as we discussed, with the supporting player receiving the ball while facing the boundary.

Your players have to empathize with their teammates. They have to give a pass that they'd like to receive, and believe me, everyone would rather receive the ball facing the field than facing the sideline. In moments like this, you need to freeze play, recreate the event and ask the passer how it could have turned out better. This is another little big thing. Everyone's life is easier when they can receive the ball facing the field.

In this diagram, the ball is being played into space for a supporting player to run onto. The weight of this pass will determine which way the supporting player will be facing when she receives the ball. This is a common occurrence in possession games.

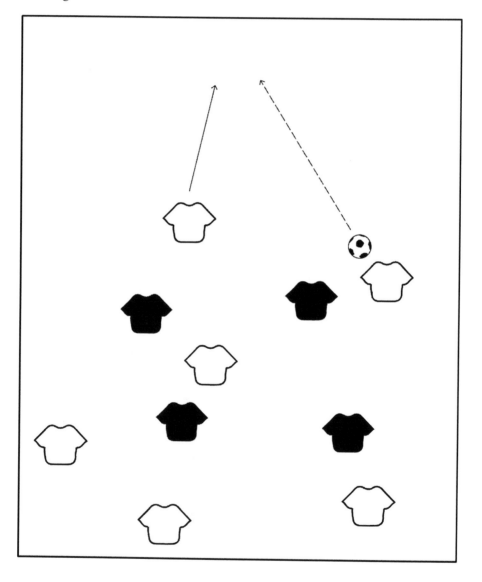

20

The Next Pass

In the *What's Next* chapter we discussed knowing what a player is going to do before she receives the ball. Now we're talking about looking even a little further into the future.

The next pass is the pass that follows the one I'm about to play. Before I pass the ball, I've got to evaluate the pass that should come after mine. I've got to look at my target's situation and assess where *her* pass should go. I've got to ask myself, "Who should she pass to?" Then I've got provide a pass that helps her execute. It's no longer about playing to the proper foot solely to protect the ball. Now it's about playing to the proper foot regardless of whether or not my target is under pressure. It's about giving her the best chance to play her next pass quickly and successfully.

We've all heard about chess masters who are thinking 3 moves ahead; this is the same concept. The pass I give should talk. If I play it into your left side, it should be because I've assessed the situation and recognized that your next pass should be in that direction. My pass is telling you that you need to go left.

For your team to keep the ball, the players need to understand that merely getting the ball to a teammate isn't good enough. They've got to get the ball to their teammates in a way that sets up the next movement, and doing that requires them to start processing the bigger picture.

This concept isn't the easiest thing in the world for a lot of players to understand, but with repetition, they will improve. One-touch exercises are excellent for developing this idea because the receiver of the pass doesn't get a touch to clean up the ball. That means it's the passer's responsibility to put her teammate in a position to connect the next pass. As we like to say, 'Your pass is her first touch.'

Here's the good news: When the bulk of your players get the hang of this, you're doing something right. Factoring in the next pass will greatly improve your team's speed of play and in turn, help you keep the ball.

SECTION 2
INDIVIDUAL
POSSESSION

21

One of Them

Possession soccer isn't always a tidy run of quick passes. Yeah, we all pine for those runs of nine consecutive one-touch passes where we ping combinations around a befuddled opponent, but our teams don't live in that world; they just visit it occasionally. To get to those moments or to keep one of those passing runs alive, you need players who are going to win their individual battles. You need players who can receive the ball under heavy pressure and find their way out of it. Regardless of how pretty you'd like your team to play, the game is often determined in the trenches where individual battles are fought.

Even if your players completely buy into the idea of playing the simple pass quickly, there are going to be many, many times when that's just not an option. Eventually there comes a time and place when a player is going to have to solve pressure on her own. She's going to be under heavy pressure with no immediate support from her teammates, and she's going to have to get out of that jam all by herself. At times like this, her ability to stay composed and escape pressure on the dribble will determine whether or not your team keeps the ball. As much as you may want to your players to pass, pass, pass, their ability to dribble themselves out of pressure is critical to your team's possession.

One of my coaching mottos is this: *It takes more than one of them to take the ball from one of us.* That means my players are expected to be able to protect the ball from a single pressuring opponent. If we habitually turn the ball over to a single opponent, we're going to lose a lot of games. Players must be able to break this type of pressure on their own, and they do that through a combination of shielding and escaping.

The next two chapters include exercises that will help your players improve their ability to solve pressure from a single opponent.

22

Shielding

I typically begin a shielding progression by having the players pair off with one ball to each pair. The pairs spread themselves out around the field to avoid collisions. One player starts with the ball; the other is the defender. Then I simply say, "Your objective is to shield the ball from your opponent. If she wins it, her job is to shield it from you. Whoever has the ball at the end of 30 seconds is the winner. Go!"

And what we end up with is a circus. There are always a few pairs that end up in a different zip code from where they began. That's because a lot of players don't understand the difference between shielding and dribbling. A player feels pressure on one side of her body and her reflex reaction is to dribble away from that pressure. But that's not shielding.

The key to shielding is to protect the ball *and* hold your ground. If you're not holding your ground, you're not shielding, you're dribbling. Teach your players to welcome the physical contact and to stay composed under heavy pressure. You don't want to concede ground without a fight.

I explain this to them and we play the game a few more times, and it gets a lot better. But to challenge them further, it's a good idea to put them into a confined space. So the next step of the progression is the shielding box.

Shielding Box — 10x10 yard grid. Player A starts with the ball and her opponent, Player B, on her back. The game is 30 seconds long. Whoever has the ball at the end of 30 seconds is the winner. If one player knocks the ball out of bounds, the opponent gets to restart with a free dribble into the grid. Emphasize heavy physical contact from the pressuring player. Allow shirt-grabbing and pushing. This game should be a war.

The final piece of this progression is the 10-second game. You can do it in or out of the grids; it really doesn't matter. In this game, Player A starts with possession of the ball. She takes a shielding stance with the outside of her foot about six inches away from the ball. This puts her sideways to her opponent, Player B. Player B then must lean on Player A. There must be physical contact between the two bodies before you begin. When you start the game, Player A must protect the ball from Player B without touching it. If either player touches the ball, Player B wins. Player A's objective is to protect the ball without touching it for 10 seconds.

Coaching Points for 1v1 Shielding Exercises
- Stay composed. Welcome the contact.
- Stay sideways to the defender and use a wide stance to put distance between the defender and the ball.
- Use your arm to build a cage to keep the defender away.
- Lean hard into the defender.
- Take as few touches as possible. Many players want to start a love affair between the ball and the soles of their feet. Use your body to protect the ball; move the ball only when it will actually benefit you.

23

Escaping

Escaping means dribbling to escape pressure. It's far different than dribbling to beat and get behind an opponent. For example, a player may have to escape when she receives the ball facing her own goal with heavy pressure on her back. Often in these situations, a player will have to combine escaping technique with shielding to break pressure.

One of my favorite drills for escaping is the Escape Tunnel. I like this game because it's a pretty realistic re-creation of a game situation where an attacker has pressure tight on her back. Plus, you can further challenge the attacker by having a server chip or bounce balls into the grid from different angles. Before you incorporate this drill, let me tell you the four most common mistakes your players are going to make.

Mistake #1 – They'll take their first touch directly away from the defender. In an effort to avoid the opponent on her back, a player will reflexively take her first touch in the opposite direction of where she wants to go, and then she'll start thinking about how to escape the pressuring opponent. We don't want to concede any more ground than necessary, so let's find a better way. Angling her touch toward one side or another is often a better option.

Mistake #2 – They won't pre-fake. There's nothing wrong with throwing in a fake before you touch the ball. This is an excellent way to unbalance an aggressive defender. A little twist of the hips or a dip of the shoulder can get the defender leaning one way, leaving you the chance to escape in the other direction.

Mistake #3 – They'll touch the ball every time they change direction with their bodies. Every time they move, they'll feel obligated to touch the ball and it'll look like a Coerver clinic. It's okay to fake one direction, leave the ball where it is and then go back to it when you explode out of your fake. As a matter of fact, this is often when the battle is won. This is a hard point to make in print, but if you do this exercise with your team, you'll see what I mean.

Mistake #4 – They'll rush. They'll be in such a hurry to try to get out of the grid that they'll become very predictable. I tell the players not to rush and to enjoy their time on the ball. Composure is a vital element to escaping pressure. This exercise will help develop it.

Escape Tunnel 1

The attacking player starts with the ball between her feet and the defender on her back. The defending player pokes the ball into the grid and play is live. (Make sure the defender gently pokes the ball into the middle of the grid, otherwise the attacker is going to start pinned up against the boundary). If the ball leaves the grid, the defender wins. The attacker wins by dribbling, not shooting, through the gates on the starting line.

Escape Tunnel 2

Now the game starts with a serve from someone outside the grid. You can vary the server's starting point as indicated by the balls in the diagram. You can also mix in flighted or bouncing serves.

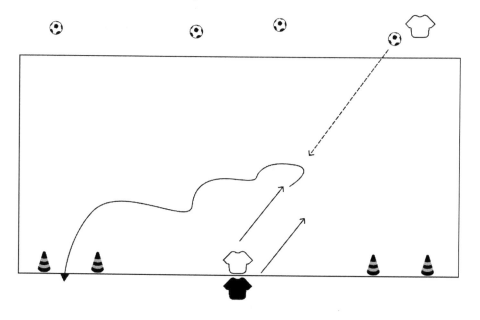

Three Man

This is a combination of shielding and escaping. You'll need a good bit of space to do this with an entire team because there are no boundaries. Establish groups of three. Designate an attacker, defender and server. The server starts with the ball. The attacker is next to her with the defender on her back. The server pushes a 10-15 yard pass out in front of the attacker. The attacker's objective is to get to the ball, escape pressure and return the ball with an accurate pass to the server. The server immediately pushes a one-touch pass in another direction and the game goes on. If the defender wins the ball, she becomes the attacker. Play for 45-90 seconds. This is a high-intensity game, so a good bit of fitness is also incorporated.

1v1 + Targets

The grid is 20x10. Each round lasts one minute. (You can also play this game 2v2 or more; just make the grid bigger. This is an excellent possession/combination game at 2v2 and 3v3.)

Inside the grid it's 1v1. Outside each end of the grid there is a neutral target player. The target players may not enter the grid and the combatants may not leave it.

We'll give the targets a two-touch restriction to start. In later rounds we'll limit them to one touch. The target players' job is to stay active along the end-lines to support the player on the ball, and to return the ball to the player who passed it to them.

To start, designate one of the players in the grid to start with the ball. That player gets a point each time he gets the ball into a target. He can play into the same target with consecutive passes, but he only gets a point for the first one. After that he must play into the other target to earn a point. If the opponent wins the ball, that player assumes the attacking role and tries to connect passes into either target. In short, whoever has the ball is the attacker.

One rule worth considering is to permit the target players to pass directly to one another. The value of allowing the target-to-target pass is that it gives the attacking player the chance to drag the defender out of the seam to set up the penetrating pass. This is quite a useful piece of soccer savvy when you're actually playing games. The downside of that rule is that it forces the defender to remain centrally when a target has the ball. This means that by slipping out to a wider angle, the attacker can typically receive the ball under less pressure. My advice is to allow target-to-target pass when the targets are under a one-touch restriction, and to disallow it otherwise.

I like this game because it forces the attacking player to break pressure *and* advance the ball, then immediately move to support the target's next pass. This game helps a player to develop his composure under pressure and his ability to craft his way out of a jam.

Incidentally, because I use a number of drills that employ targets, let me re-emphasize the importance of making sure your target players stay active. Target players have a habit of going catatonic, but in reality, they should be constantly in motion to provide good passing angles. As you run your exercise, keep one eye on the targets and demand that they stay active.

1v1 + Targets

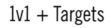

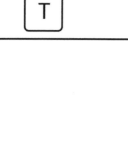

3-Ball

3-Ball is a pretty chaotic game that incorporates a lot of shielding and escaping. It also hits a lot of other important topics such as vision, communication, winning restarts and defending to dispossess an opponent (as opposed to just poking it away or tackling it out of bounds). This game often puts players in a situation where they have to solve 1v1 or 1v2 pressure on their own. The player on the ball has to assess her situation and decide whether she should attempt to pass the ball to a teammate or take on the responsibility of protecting it from a single opponent.

It's 4v4 in a 15x20 yd. grid. You can also play 5v5 or 6v6 and adjust the grid size as necessary. Have plenty of spare balls scattered around the outside of the grid. Each team starts with a ball. A few seconds after the game begins, roll another ball onto the field. After 60 seconds, the team with at least two of the balls wins. If a player knocks the ball out of the grid, the opponent is allowed to restart with a free dribble into the grid. Many times there will be at least one ball out of play at the 60-second mark. I never stop the game until all three balls are on the field. I usually play a best of five series.

3-Ball

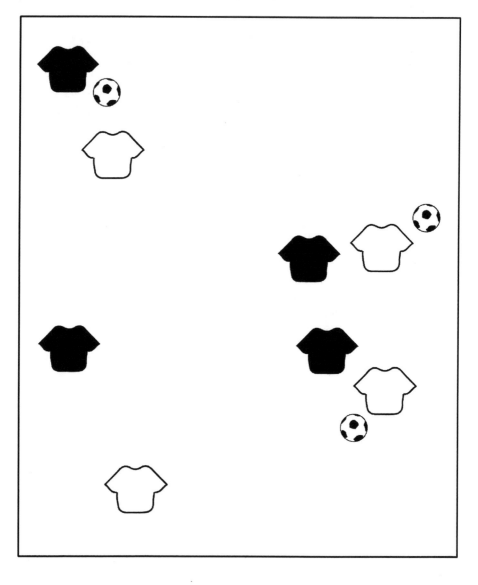

Checkers

Checkers is a tight space game of 6v6 divided into four smaller games of 2v1 or 1v2. You'll take a 24x24 yard grid and divide it into four smaller grids of 12x12. When you first introduce this game to your team, you may want to extend the grids to 15x15. In two of the small grids, Team A enjoys a numerical advantage. In the other two grids, Team A is outnumbered.

The players may not leave their grids, but the ball can travel from one grid to another. The objective is to maneuver the ball into all four grids without conceding possession. Every time a team does that, it scores a point. This is a very difficult game because the space is tight and the players will naturally gravitate toward the center where the four small grids intersect. You've got to coach the team with the ball to stay disciplined in their spacing and to stay active to look for passing seams.

This is one of those games that won't run smoothly because it's very difficult to score points, but you'll get a lot of smaller victories as the players develop and demonstrate their composure. The critical element to this game is that a team doesn't concede the ball in the grids where it has a numerical advantage. Enjoying a 2v1 advantage means a responsibility to stay composed and not be dispossessed by a single opponent.

Checkers

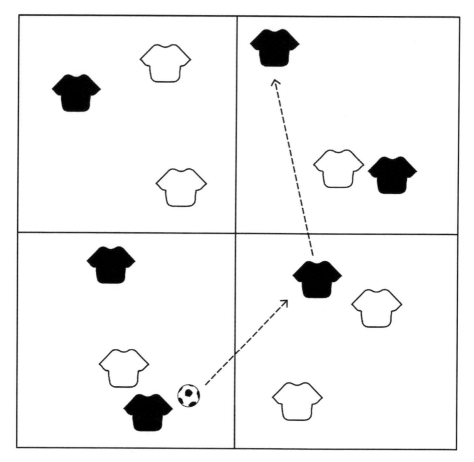

SECTION 3
SMALL NUMBERS
POSSESSION

24

The Small Numbers Progression

Now that the players feel more comfortable protecting the ball during their 1v1 battles, it's time to muddy the waters and add more moving pieces. Now we're talking about passing quickly as our first option, and escaping as Plan B. And we are going to start at the very beginning.

The small numbers progression is very basic, but it establishes the foundation for teaching your team to keep the ball. It involves passing to the proper foot; receiving with the proper foot; putting proper weight on our passes; giving good angles; playing quickly and playing to good numbers and away from bad ones; and empathy. Whenever it's time to introduce possession, I always start with this progression, regardless of how talented the players may be. Nobody is too good to skip the basics.

Progression Part 1 – 4v0

We're going to start with a game of 4v0 in a grid that's 10x10 yards. Each player starts in a corner and stays in that corner for the duration of the exercise. Player A starts with the ball and passes it to Player B. Player B receives it and passes it to Player C. Player C receives it and passes it to Player D and so on and the ball just keeps going around the grid. The only restrictions are that every player must take two touches, and the players may only touch the ball with the inside of their right foot (until we change directions in Round 2).

To execute this properly, players must open up their bodies and receive the ball across their standing leg. Because a lot of the passes will be less than perfect, the receiving player will have to make a lot of small, quick adjustments. I usually have them do this for 1.5 minutes and then we switch the direction of the ball, so now the players may only pass and receive with the inside of the left foot.

Then we go back to the right foot and turn it into a 45-second game where the players are competing against all the other grids. Each completed pass is worth one point, but the players still must adhere to the restrictions. If the ball leaves the grid or a player breaks a restriction, subtract a point. You'll see the balls moving around the grids with a lot more pace. You'll also see a lot more mistakes.

4v0

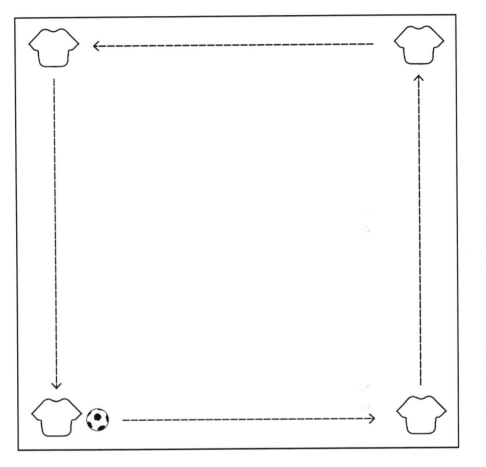

Progression Part 2 – 3v0

Now we're just going to subtract one player from each grid and play 3v0. The ball travels the same direction for the duration of the round and we'll keep the same restrictions. Here the difference is that we have to incorporate some timing, because the passer of the ball is always playing to the empty corner. This is basically a more fluid version of the 'Letter L' exercise we introduced earlier.

Ideally, the player receiving the ball is arriving to the empty corner at full steam at the same time as the ball. Now she has to make a much more difficult adjustment to open her hips and receive the ball across her standing leg. We'll ask the passer to take a little weight off the pass, but not much. Like I said, the key to this one is the timing, so the passer has to delay her pass until her teammate is about halfway across the grid. If she doesn't, the ball will roll right through the empty corner. By that same token, if the supporting player begins her run too early, she'll be standing in the corner before the ball arrives and that's no good either. This is the bigger problem you'll run into.

This drill will not go smoothly at first because the player who should receive the next pass will almost always leave too soon. I'm not sure why that is, but you can take it to the bank. You have to make this exercise choppy at first. Make the supporting player hold her run until the player before her has received the ball and gotten balanced and ready to play the next pass. Once they get the hang of holding their run, then you can let it go a little more freely and they'll start to develop a nice rhythm. When your players get comfortable with the mechanics of this exercise, turn it into a competition between the grids like we did in 4v0.

The point of this exercise is to teach players to open their hips, receive the ball across their standing leg and face the field – all while moving at top speed. It also gets them into the habit of moving to give a great passing angle, which becomes more important in the next exercise.

3v0

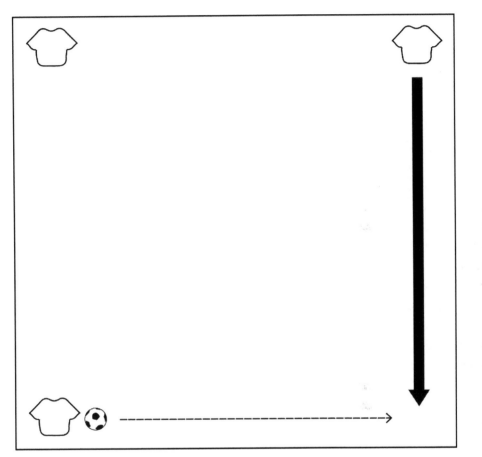

Progression Part 3 – 3v1

Now we're going to introduce a defender and play 3v1. This is where a lot of coaches choose to begin their possession progressions. I think you're better off breaking it down into even smaller bits as we did in parts 1 and 2.

3v1 is a simple game. In that same 10x10 grid (or smaller), now the three attackers play keep-away from the defender. Whoever gives the ball away trades places with the defender.

In addition to the pressuring defender, there's one other big difference from our last exercise: Now the ball can change directions on the fly. That means that the supporting players actually have to read the pressure on the ball and make decisions about where they need to support. The player on the ball will typically still be in one of the corners, and that player needs support at the corners closest to her – the ones that form a right angle with her in the middle. In other words, we don't want a supporting player to take up a position in the corner that is diagonal from the player on the ball. That means if two of the players play a series of consecutive passes back and forth, the third attacker needs to be making tracks back and forth across the opposite side of the grid.

There are several restrictions you can add to spice up this game. You can put on a one or two-touch restriction or specify that if the ball stops dead at an attacker's feet, the play is dead and she becomes the defender.

The 3v1 exercise heavily emphasizes close support, which is an essential element to keeping the ball as a team. The players have to work hard to support the player on the ball, even if the next pass isn't to them. In my experience, the determination of the players off the ball to get to a proper passing angle is a major coaching point in this exercise. Then, once the ball comes their way, are they handling it properly by opening up and receiving it across their standing leg when possible and prudent? To be good at big-picture possession, your team has to first be great at small-picture possession, and that requires a heavy emphasis on proper habits. That's why we do this drill. We play 3v1 to instill proper habits of close support and passing and receiving.

If your team is playing this well, the players will be panting. This should be a physically demanding exercise. If the players aren't breathing hard after a few minutes, then they aren't working hard enough to get to their supporting angles.

3v1

In the diagram, as the ball is passed to the attacker in the lower right corner, the teammate in the upper left sprints across to support her. The attacker on the ball should always have support at both ends of the 90 degree angle.

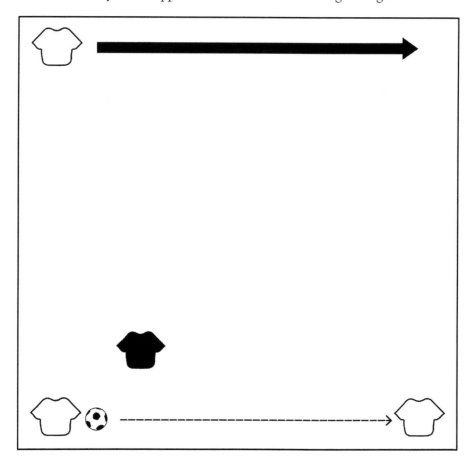

Progression Part 4 – 5v2

Now we're going to make the space a bit bigger – 10x15 yards – and move into 5v2. As with any of these exercises, make the space tighter if the players need a loftier challenge.

In case you're not familiar with 5v2, it's another monkey-in-the-middle game and the rules are pretty much the same as 3v1. When an attacker is responsible for losing the ball, she trades spots with the defender who has been in the middle the longest.

5v2 is another close-support exercise, but it adds a couple of new dimensions to our game of keep-away. There's now a second defender that the attacking players have to account for, and now there's the opportunity to play a penetrating pass that splits those defenders.

The second defender means that there will be pressure on the ball more quickly, so the attacking players have to be cleaner technically and must move more quickly to provide proper passing angles. Playing to the proper foot and receiving with the proper foot are now even more important. Additionally, the attacking players must start putting more thought into the next pass, as in, the pass after their own pass. The pass that eliminates the first defender won't necessarily eliminate the second one, so to keep the ball as a group, the attackers must evaluate the situation of the teammate receiving their pass.

The problem you'll encounter in 5v2 is that the supporting players are prone to get a little bit lazy. This is where you'll notice the supporting players not moving with enough conviction to offer the very best passing angle and therefore, you'll see a lot of passes being received with the wrong foot. More often than not, one step will turn a lazy angle into a good angle. You've got to demand that the supporting players stay extremely active to provide excellent passing angles. This is where you may want to introduce the 3-step rule.

My greatest pet peeve in this exercise is that the players on the side of the grid opposite the ball will often go catatonic. Those players need to stay switched on and remain active. They should be constantly in motion making little adjustments to find passing seams. The most effective pass in 5v2 is the penetrating pass that splits the defenders because it breaks their pressure and forces them to reorganize. Plus it damages their collective will to chase. If the players opposite the ball aren't working, you miss opportunities to split the defenders. More importantly, sometimes the split is the only option for the player on the ball. And nothing in 5v2 gnaws at me more than a pass that splits the two defenders then rolls out the far side of the grid. Clearly the seam was there, so why wasn't the support? My rule is that in these situations, the passer of the ball doesn't go into the middle, the player who should've filled that seam does.

Incidentally, that's something you need to consider as you coach possession exercises. Often times possession isn't lost because the pass was bad; it's lost because a supporting player gave a lazy angle. Keep an eye out for those moments and hold the supporting player accountable by making her become the defender. When we get into bigger-picture possession games, you can hold an entire team accountable for one player's lazy angle. I do it all the time and believe me, it sends a much stronger message when a group of teammates have to pay for your sins.

Bonus Tip: We use 5v2 as a warm-up nearly every day – 3.5 minutes of two-touch followed by 3.5 minutes of one-touch. Doing the same routine every day can become a bit dull and when the players get bored, they are less enthusiastic about making the necessary runs to support, so the standard suffers. Steve Holeman invented a brilliant scoring system to spice things up. We call it the 5v2 ladder.

We typically have three grids playing 5v2, and the grids are numbered 1, 2 and 3. Every player is responsible for tracking the number of times she had to go in the middle. At the end of the day, we tally up everyone's score. The next day, the two players with the most giveaways in Grid 1 are relegated to Grid 2.

The same applies to relegating players from Grid 2 to 3. The two players with the fewest giveaways in Grid 3 are promoted to Grid 2, and the two best from Grid 2 are promoted to Grid 1. The objective for each player is to reach Grid 1 and stay there for as long as possible. (More days than not there'll be some ties, so you just have to create your own tie-breaking system.)

We track the results over the entirety of the season. Not only does this motivate the players to maintain a high standard, but it also encourages the players to hold their teammates accountable, as in, *'That pass should've been to my left foot!'* and *'I'm not going in because of your bad pass!'* Believe me, when we introduced the ladder, our 5v2 warm-ups got noticeably more intense.

Some players are just better than others and those players will take up residence in Grid 1 with an occasional visit to Grid 2. What was astonishing to me was that over the course of an entire season, we had some players who never made it to Grid 1. This gave us the chance to give those players a bit of an awakening about their levels of focus. All it takes to reach Grid 1 is two good days in a row. Any player is capable of that, but it requires a concentrated effort. When a player can't string together two good days in a row over the course of entire season, it forces her to look in the mirror about her level of effort.

5v2

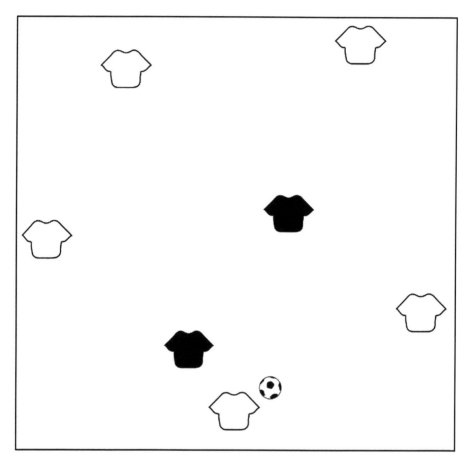

Progression Part 5 - Dutch

The final step of this progression is the Dutch Game. This game involves three teams, with two of the teams playing keep-away from the third. Let's say the red and blue teams are playing keep-away from yellow. If red gives the ball away to yellow, blue and yellow are immediately playing keep-away from red. When introducing this game, I would start with three players per team on a field that is 35 x 20. This is a big space and will need to be pared down as your players improve. Have lots of extra balls surrounding the grid so play can be restarted quickly when the ball goes out of bounds.

This is a fun game once the players start to figure it out. The quick changes in the roles of the teams (attacking or defending) forces the players to stay alert. Often times the ball will be turned over several times in succession, so the players have to figure out which team is the one defending.

In Dutch we incorporate all of the elements of possession. The space is bigger so we can incorporate some longer passes. The players can move more freely so we'll see some combinations. Discipline in spacing becomes critical to keeping possession. And now the ability to recognize good numbers or bad numbers becomes very important.

I believe that it's a good idea to occasionally over-coach these possession exercises. That means I'll start and stop and correct and restart constantly, particularly when introducing a new exercise. It will be very choppy by design because until the players understand how possession needs to work, this game will be a mess. So when one player receives the ball I'll have everyone freeze. Then I'll have the defenders position themselves wherever they want and then freeze them in those spots. Then I'll have the attacking players adjust to the defenders and run to the spots where they want to be and freeze them as well. A lot of them will be giving less than great angles, so I'll correct them. I'll look for players who aren't offering a great angle, or aren't offering the proper foot, or who are standing a step inside the boundary when they should be standing directly on it. I'll hammer away at every little detail until everyone is properly positioned. Then I'll have the player on the ball connect a pass and then I'll freeze everyone again and the whole process will start anew. Like I said, it's choppy. But I'm going to do what I have to do to flatten out that learning curve.

When you introduce this game, you should be prepared to over-coach. One area that will require plenty of correction is the spacing. All the players are going to gravitate toward the ball and they'll make your nice big space way too small. Remember the story about the egg. When you're in possession, you want the opponent to have to cover a lot of ground.

Good spacing is goes hand in hand with counting. Dutch is the first exercise we've introduced where the defending team can be broken into big and little parts. For example, if two players from the defending team are pressuring the ball, that means there's only one player left to defend the rest of the field. The attacking players need to be able to recognize this and play where the numbers are best. In that same vein, Dutch offers players the chance to break pressure with a flighted pass. That's requires good spacing and at least one player with the discipline to break free of the ball's magnetic pull.

One of the other issues you'll need to address often in the early stages is support in the middle of the field. You'll notice many times that all of the attacking players have been sucked to the field's perimeter, leaving no one to support from the middle. You always want someone supporting in the middle. That player is often the one who can turn and break pressure and move the ball from bad numbers to good ones. It's a smart idea to have a central midfielder spending time in there, but there will be times when she has to vacate the middle. When the middle is vacated, it's up to another attacking player to recognize the situation and fill that space.

When the middle is left empty, I'll freeze the game and ask the players, "What's wrong with this picture?" After they hear the answer a few times, they start recognizing the problem on their own and a few enterprising players will look for opportunities to fill the middle. This is a good thing.

Incidentally, since we're on the topic of supporting in the middle, Dutch is a great game for introducing the concept of supporting behind the fence. That middle player will have ample opportunities to play in front of the fence or behind it. It's your chance to show her the value of playing behind it.

Dutch is a great way to finish the progression because it clouds the picture much more than the previous exercises, but the attackers still enjoy a 2:1 numerical advantage, so there are lots of opportunities for success. As the players get better at understanding where to support and playing to the proper foot and playing away from bad numbers, you'll start to see some nice passing rhythms. When you come back to this exercise in subsequent sessions, start focusing more on the advanced concepts like speed of play and the next pass. Once the players are comfortable with the exercise, introduce the three-step rule.

One very advanced and confusing variation to this exercise is to add a stipulation that the players can only pass to a player on the other attacking team. For example, if red and blue are the attacking teams, red players can only pass to blue ones and vise-versa. To succeed under this stipulation, the players' brains have to be working at warp speed. The game will be a mess for quite a while, but it's a good way to liven up the party every now and then.

There are plenty of ways to score the Dutch game, but my favorite variation is 31. I love 31 because it's about risk management, specifically, when to play one-touch and when to take two or more touches. We want our teams to play quickly, not rushed, so we need players who recognize the times to hold the ball as well as when to play with just one touch. 31 rewards players for making the proper decisions. It's a tough game to keep track of, so if you have some helpers or injured players available (preferably three), call them into service and assign a team to each one of them.

In 31, there is no touch restriction, but whenever a player on either of the two attacking teams successfully passes the ball to any other attacking player with one touch, *both* attacking teams are credited with a point. To clarify, two teams get credit for every point that is scored. The object of the game is to be the first team to score 31 points. I incorporate this scoring system (points for one-touch passes) into a lot of possession exercises.

DUTCH

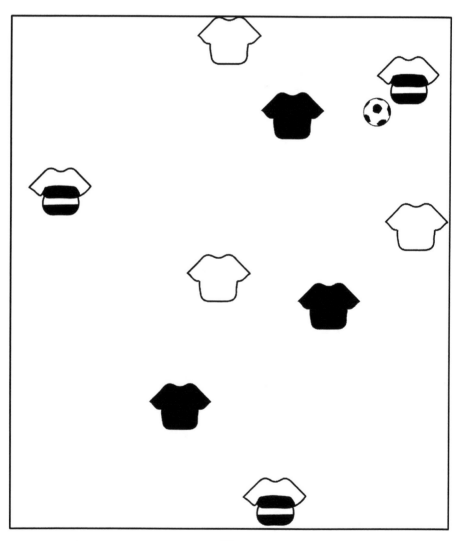

SECTION 4
SMALL AREA
POSSESSION
EXERCISES

25

Small Area Possession Exercises

T he exercises we covered in the possession progression have been the best tools I've found for teaching the fundamentals of keeping the ball. I'm not saying I invented them or that that they are the most dynamic; I'm just saying that they work for me. And since I'm not that smart, they should work for you too. But they aren't the only possession exercises out there.

There are more possession exercises than I can count, and once your players get a solid handle on how to keep the ball and why you're keeping it, it's a good idea to mix in other exercises to keep them excited and to further challenge them. The rest of this book is a collection of possession exercises. Believe me, there are many, many others. These are just my favorites. Feel free to adjust them as necessary and add your own restrictions and improve upon them any way you like. I hope they serve you well.

6-3-1

In a grid 15x20, seven attackers play keep-away from three defenders for one straight minute. One target attacker is designated to stay in the central area of the grid. Attackers score a point every time they get the ball into that attacker. In this game, it's important for the attacking players to get the ball into the target's proper foot to set up the next pass. One variation is to limit the designated attacker to two touches and all the other attackers to one touch, or vise-versa.

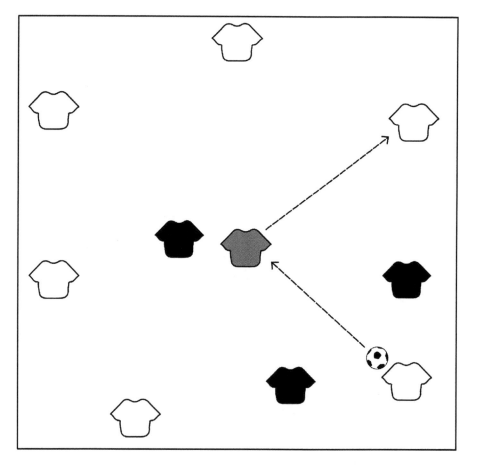

6-3-1 Rush

This is a game that emphasizes a high speed of play in close quarters.

Make a grid that's 15x15 or smaller. Divide into two teams of seven players. The red team starts in the grid and will be the attacking team for 90 seconds. Make sure one of the red players takes up a central position. The blue team starts at one corner, outside of the grid. All of the balls start with the coach. The game begins when the coach knocks a ball into a red player. At that moment, three blues come rushing into the grid to defend. Their objective is to knock the ball out of the grid. Every time the red team strings five consecutive passes, it scores a point. Every time the ball leaves the grid, the blue team replaces its three players with three new ones and a new ball is immediately served in to the red team. This is a physically demanding game and requires a lot of hard work from the defending team. By that same token, because the defending trio will always arrive on the field at a full sprint, a fast speed of play is required of the attacking team.

This is not a great exercise for making coaching points because the pace is so frantic. In 6-3-1 Rush, the game is the teacher, and the students are learning how to move the ball in a tight space under heavy pressure.

6-3-1 Rush

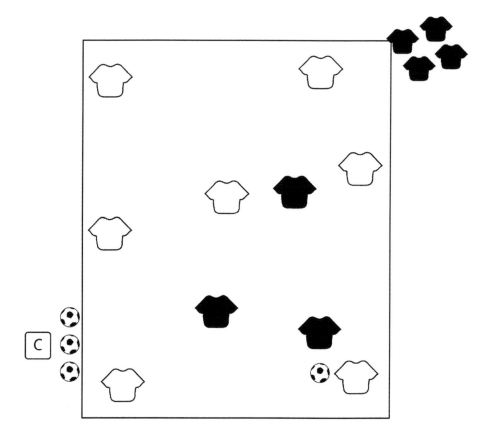

2v2 + Neutral Wingers

Grid size is 20x10. There are two teams of two players plus two neutral wingers. The objective of this game is to stop the ball on the opponent's end-line. The wingers may not enter the grid and the combatants may not leave the grid. The wingers may move freely up and down their lines and they play for whichever team has the ball. I typically limit the wingers to one touch but there's no harm in starting with a two-touch restriction.

This isn't a typical possession game because there is no reward for stringing a certain number of passes together. The reason I like this game is that puts a high value on spatial awareness. As shown in the diagram, it is common for players to clog their own team's passing seams, particularly when one of the wingers has the ball. In the diagram, one of the attackers is directly between the winger with the ball and the weak-side winger. When two players fill the same seam, then two players are doing a job that one player could do and the other player is either in the way or unavailable.

The team in possession must remember that this game is actually 4v2 and the players need to move in such a way that they maintain their numerical advantage. When two players are filling the same seam, one of those players gets nullified and the numbers shrink to 3v2 or even 2v2. So even while trying to advance the ball up the grid to score, the players need to maintain some semblance of team shape. The wingers provide width by default, so it's particularly important that the middle players provide depth. Because the field is so tight, this requires a lot of quick movements to find good passing seams, so there should be a frequent interchange of attacking roles from the players inside the grid.

As we discussed earlier, when two players occupy the same seam, the player furthest from the ball must be the one to dictate the shape because she has the best view of the whole picture. In this exercise, it's not typically a vertical seam that gets clogged but a lateral one. In the diagram, it's up to the weak-side winger to either move to a new angle or to kick the attacking player out of that seam.

In this drill, you'll actually have moments when a winger has the ball and all four attacking players will form a straight line. That means that the player closest to the ball has cut out her two teammates and the game has become 2v2. This is a great chance to freeze the picture and explain how the attackers are failing to mind their shape and maintain their two-player advantage.

2v2 + Neutral Wingers

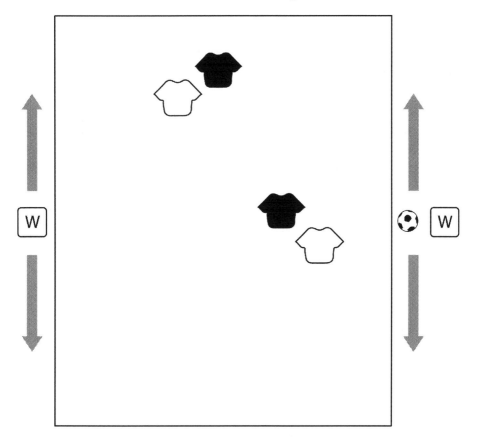

Cross the River

Cross the River is a mobilized version of 5v2. Make a grid that is roughly 30x15, then divide it into three smaller grids of 10x15. Have a server with plenty of soccer balls stationed just wide of the middle grid. Divide into two teams of five. In one of the end grids, start with five reds playing keep-away from two blues. The middle grid is empty. The final grid has the remaining three blue players.

The attacking team scores by stringing together five consecutive passes. There is no limit to the amount of points they can score on any given turn. If they connect 20 consecutive passes before losing the ball, they score four points. The defending team's objective is to knock the ball out of the grid as quickly as possible. As soon as the ball leaves the grid, the coach sends a new ball down to the grid with the three blues. Their teammates race back to that grid to support them, as do two red players who will serve as defenders. That leaves three reds waiting in the initial grid. Now the blues are trying to score points. When the ball leaves the blues' grid, the coach serves the next ball into the grid with the three reds, and the game plays on like that.

This is another game that incorporates a good bit of fitness.

Cross the River

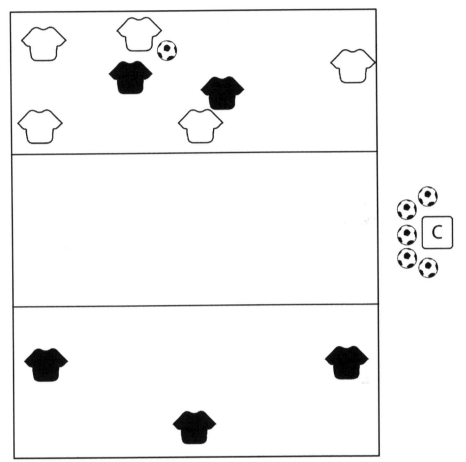

Border Patrol

This is a fast-paced game similar to Cross the River, but we're adding a third team. Divide into three teams of six (you can also play this with teams of four). Set up a grid that is 50x15. Then divide that grid into three smaller grids. The two end grids will be 20x15, and the middle grid will be 10x15.

Put the red team in one of the end grids and the blue team in the other end grid. The yellow team starts in the middle grid. The coach stands just wide of the middle grid with plenty of balls. The team in the middle grid (yellow) is the defending team. The game starts when the coach serves a ball into the red team. The yellow team sends three players into that grid to defend, while the remaining three yellows stay in the middle grid.

The red team's objective is to pass the ball through or over the middle grid and into the blue team. If they do that successfully, the get a point, but they can't play that pass until they've connected at least five passes. Also, the three yellows in the middle grid will be trying to block that pass.

If the reds successfully connect the pass into the blues, the three yellows in the middle grid run into the blues' grid to defend, and the three yellows who were just chasing in the red grid slide into the middle grid. Now the blues are trying to connect at least five passes and get the ball back across to the reds.

Let's go back to our original scenario that had the reds playing keep-away from the yellows. If the ball leaves the grid, the play is dead. So let's say the yellows tipped the ball out of the grid. Immediately the coach would serve the next ball into the blues. The six reds would vacate their end grid and the six yellows would replace them. Three of the reds would sprint into the blues' grid to defend, and three of them would take up positions in the middle grid.

One of the things I like about Cross the River and Border Patrol is that a loss of possession instantly results in a form of punishment, namely a sprint to defend. Believe me, that gets old in a hurry, particularly if you aren't the player who actually gave away the ball, so players are less likely to tolerate careless mistakes from their teammates. This results in a higher concentration level from the players in possession. We've already discussed selling the *why* to your players, and games like these can help you. They give you the chance to emphasize how much more fun soccer is when your team has the ball and how much it can suck when the other team has it. Your players need to remember there is a price to be paid for giving the ball away cheaply.

Border Patrol

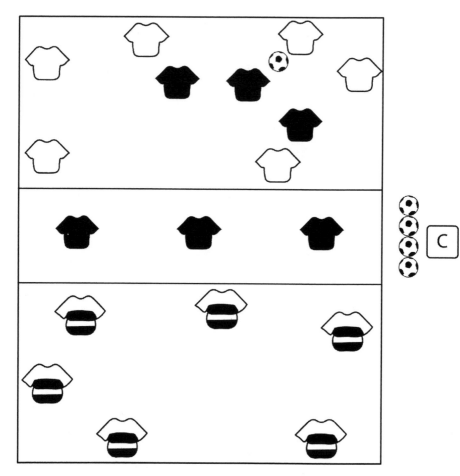

Four Corners

I'm a big fan of this game because it forces players to work hard to give solid passing angles.

The grid is 24 x 24 yards. Divide the perimeter into four smaller lines of 12 x 12. In the diagram we have a 3 v 3 + 1 neutral player inside the grid, but you can certainly play with bigger or smaller numbers. We've played this game up to 4v4 +1 in the middle with great results.

The players on the inside of the grid may not leave the grid. The players outside of the grid may not enter it.

Each team has two support players stationed on the outside of the grid, cattycorner from one another. Those players are responsible for supporting up to the midway mark on either side of their corner. They may not cut the corner. Basically they work along a right angle. These players are limited to one-touch and they may not advance past the midway point of their lines. An outside player is allowed to pass the ball to any of her teammates, and that includes passing directly to the other outside player on her team.

You can score this a couple of different ways. In one system, a team gets a point for every five passes it connects. Or you can set it up like 31, so the teams get one point for every one-touch pass they connect.

In Four Corners, the outside players have to work their tails off to give good passing angles. Because the outside players are limited to a single touch, the inside players also have to work hard to support them with good angles. *Hard work to give support* – that's how it should be, and that's why I like it. Like all possession games, Four Corners is a lot of fun once a team establishes a rhythm of possession.

Four Corners

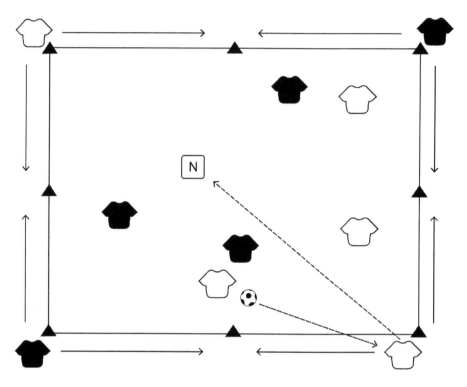

Two-Ball

Two-Ball is a crazy fun game. It's pretty chaotic, but it teaches players to keep their heads on a swivel and know what's going on behind them, and players must be constantly moving to find good passing seams. This isn't an exercise I consider a staple, but it's a nice way to mix things up every once in a while.

Start with a grid that's 30x15 and divide it into four smaller grids. The end grids will be10x15 while the two middle grids will each be 5x15. Divide into two teams of 7. In the first grid start with three reds and one blue. In the next grid three blues. Three reds in the next grid. Three blues and one red in the final grid. In each of the end grids, the team with the numerical advantage starts with a ball and plays 3v1 keep-away. To clarify, there are two balls in play simultaneously. To score a point, the attackers in the end grids must connect a pass with their teammates in the middle grid. The players in the middle grid can also connect a pass to an attacking teammate in the end grid to score a point.

The defending player in the 3v1 can win possession of the ball and knock it to her teammates, but that doesn't count as a point.

The players in the middle grid serve two purposes: they must support their attacking teammates by finding playable passing seams, and they also try to prevent their opponents from connecting passes through their grid. That means they must constantly check their shoulders to see what's going on behind them.

Whenever one team knocks a ball out of the grid, the coach serves a ball into the opponent.

An important rule in this one is that the ball cannot stop dead. If a ball stops dead at the foot of a red player, that ball is forfeited to the blue team.

Like I said, this is pretty chaotic. There will be times when one team possesses both balls and times when both balls end up in a single grid. Just roll with it. You can play first team to a certain number of points or you can play a timed game. Your call.

Two-Ball

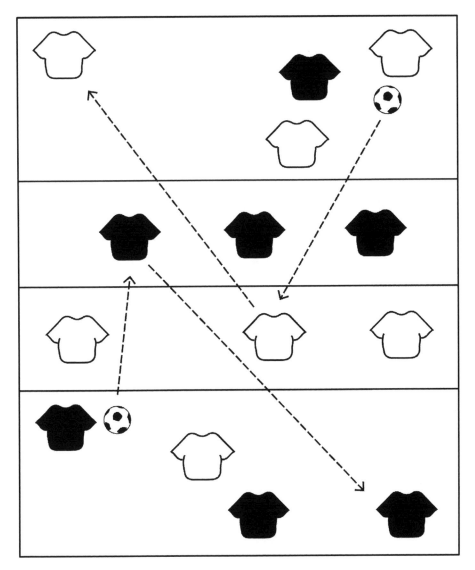

2v2 + Targets

This is the same as the 1v1 + Targets game that was introduced in the Individual Possession section. Now we are just making the field a little wider (20x15) and adding another player to each team. The same rules apply. Play rounds of 2-4 minutes.

The benefit of adding the extra players is that the players in the grid have the chance to combine with one another. This game allows us to hit many coaching points such as playing to the higher of two options, supporting underneath, playing the way we face, and a ball back for a ball forward. This game is a cool little microcosm of big-picture soccer because the players have to find a way to break pressure, either individually or in concert, to advance the ball. Additionally, it allows players to stay disciplined and not force the ball forward, as they always have an escape hatch by playing a negative ball into one of the targets.

With this one, you might want to occasionally mix in a restriction where the attacking team may not make consecutive passes into the same target. This takes away the luxury of a negative ball and forces players to solve pressure on their own more often. Either way won't kill you.

2v2 + Targets

In this diagram we see the target playing the higher of two options, which sets up a ball back for a ball forward into the advanced target.

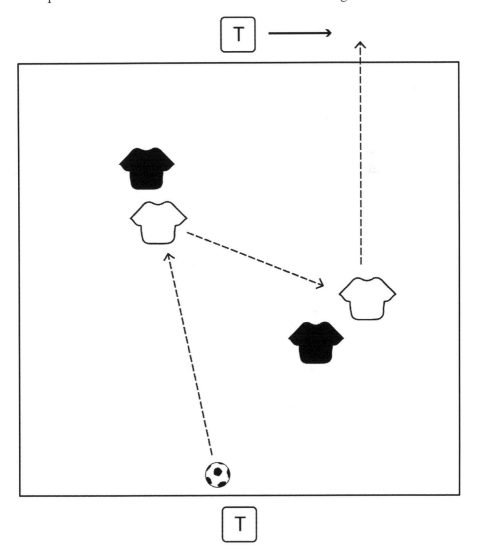

SECTION 5
BIGGER PICTURE
POSSESSION GAMES

6v6 + 1 (or 2)

Yep, nothing fancy about this one. Set up a grid that's roughly 45x25. Choose two teams of 6 plus one or two neutral players who are always on the attacking team. It's just a good, old-fashioned game of keep-away. A team scores a point every time it connects five consecutive passes. Incidentally, you can make the numbers whatever you choose (like 7v7 + 2 or 9v9 + 1). To emphasize speed of play, add a one- or two-touch restriction. I usually mix in a round where the neutral player has unlimited touches, but everyone else is limited to one touch. This restriction puts the responsibility on the neutral player to oftentimes break pressure on her own because she has the freedom of extra touches. It also forces her to work very hard to give good passing angles, because she is the escape hatch for the team with the ball.

Because the teams are close to even, this type of games forces the players to do their counting and constantly search for good numbers. These even number games are like soccer without the goals, so they're a lot more realistic than the games where the attacking team enjoys a 2:1 ratio of players. The attacking team therefore won't be as successful, but your players need to learn to keep the ball when the numbers are even. In other words, if your players can do a good job of keeping the ball in this environment, you're moving in the right direction.

I'm a fan of using a neutral player in a lot of exercises, and more often than not I'm going to select one of our center midfielders for that role. They are our playmakers so it's important for them to get a lot of touches, and it's important for their teammates to make a habit of getting them the ball. However, as a sign of their gratitude for being chosen for this luxury detail, it's critical that the neutral players actually perform well when they are handed the magic vest. The neutral player lives a charmed life because she is relieved of her defensive responsibilities, so she'd better deliver the goods on the attacking end. If the neutral player is habitually giving the ball away or not working hard to find viable passing seams, don't hesitate to swap her out with someone who will give a more inspired performance.

6v6 + 1

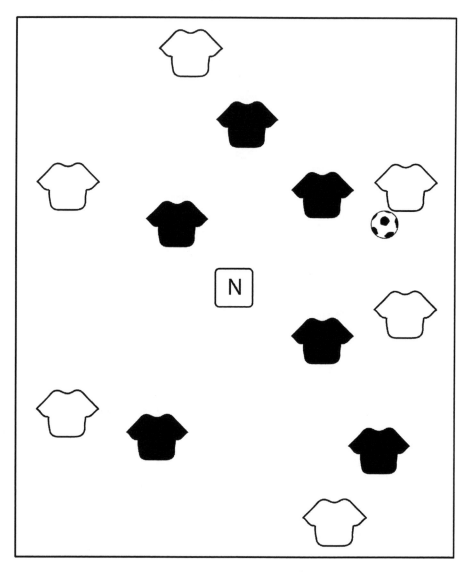

Six Goal Game (or Eight Goal Game)

Divide into two teams of seven. Add a neutral player if you like. The field is wider than it is long, roughly 40 x 45. On each end line place three mini-goals, one in the middle and one near each corner. Each team defends the goals on its own end-line and attacks the goals on the opponent's end-line. There is no offside. Five consecutive passes is worth a point. Scoring into the mini-goal is worth three points. It's important to have a rule where consecutive passes equate to goals. This forces the defending team to come out and try to win back the ball as opposed to just standing in front of their goals.

This game is a go-to drill for coaches that want to work on switching the point of attack. It involves a lot of counting and patience. If you want players to recognize good numbers from bad, this is the game for you. Often a player on the ball will start driving towards one of the wide goals and then, when the numbers turn bad, try to force a bad situation. The better option is often to turn around, then play backwards or sideways and look to attack a different goal.

A high rate of speed of play comes in handy in a game like this because the defending team will get pulled toward the goal that is under immediate threat. Quickly getting the ball to the other side of the field is how the attacking team can capitalize when the opponent gets heavy on one side. Remember when we discussed the speed of the ball as an important component in your team's speed of play? This is an exercise where the under-hit pass will stymie a potentially great attack. When the defending team gets heavy on one side, it's not enough to move the ball to the opposite side; you have to move it there *quickly*, otherwise you'll give the opponent time to recover its shape.

This is also a game where a lot of the goals result from a big, flighted ball that leaves the opponent's heavy numbers on one side of the field, exposing the side where its numbers are lighter. Big vision is a tremendous ally in this exercise.

Vertical spacing is important in this game, so make sure that the forward players stay high up the field. Because they are so used to playing with an off-side rule, they will instinctively gravitate towards their own end of the field. Remind them to keep the field big when their team has the ball.

Six Goal Game

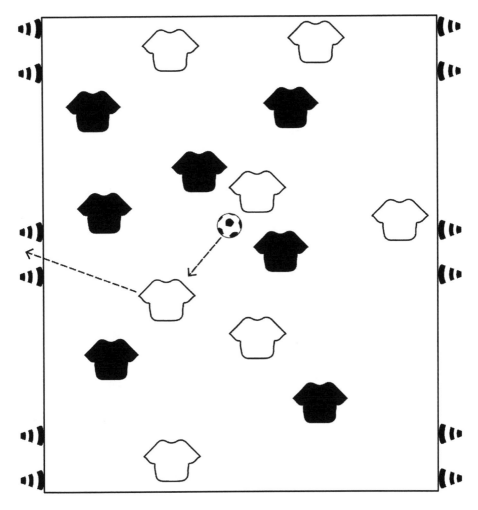

Four Target Game

You need two teams of seven players. Add a neutral player if you like. Use a grid that is 45 x 25 yards. Each team provides two target players, one for each end-line. The target players play outside of the grid; they operate under a one-touch restriction; they can move freely along their end-lines and they may not defend one another.

Inside the grid you have a game of 5v5. To score, a team must play the ball into one of its targets and that target must successfully connect the next pass. After a team scores at one end, it must attack the opposite end. If that team loses possession and then wins the ball back, it can attack to either end.

I love this game because it involves keeping possession while advancing the ball up the field. It also incorporates a lot of the higher level concepts of possession and speed of play. More than any other exercise, you'll see plenty of examples of players who should be supporting better than square but instead wander too far forward. This is a great game to teach them when to put on the brakes and support underneath. The Four Target game is an excellent arena for you to hammer home the value of a ball back for a ball forward.

Remember the chapter My Seam? This is an excellent drill to teach players to stay out of the target's seam. The ball into a target is the most important pass in this exercise, and that is the seam that will often get clogged. When that seam gets clogged, it's up to the target to tell her teammate to get the heck out of it.

Because this game is so back and forth and north and south, players need to be concerned about the next pass, particularly when playing into the target. Before a player passes to the target, she has to figure out where the target's next pass should go and then give her a fighting chance to get it there.

Targets, on the other hand, will often have the opportunity to play the higher of two options and fail miserably to do so. They'll naturally opt for the smaller, safer pass, which will frequently end up at a teammate who is five yards away and not facing the field and with no support underneath her. The target can solve a lot of her team's problems by passing to one of her higher options. Again, this will require an awareness of a lower player to stay out of a higher player's seam, so you'll get many opportunities to coach that concept.

Possession is all good and well, but you can't win if you don't move the ball up the field. This game will give you the chance to make some very valid points about playing directly into the target when the opportunity presents itself. After all, we usually don't want to play sideways if we can successfully play forward. Oftentimes the player on the ball will have a clear seam to the target but instead choose a lateral pass. This is when you tell that player that her first option should be to advance the ball up the park.

Again, because this game involves a constant search for good numbers, spacing becomes a big deal. If the red team is advancing the ball toward one end of the field, all of its players will gravitate toward that end. Even the red player who is at the back of the pack will get sucked down the field, and that makes for a crowded field. That lowest player needs to have the discipline to put on the brakes and slip away from the pack to stretch out the field, because a lot of times the way to break pressure is with a longer pass. We have to make sure she keeps the field big so that the long pass remains an option.

You can tweak this game with a lot of variations besides touch restrictions. Here are a few:

- The player who passes to the target cannot be the player who receives the target's pass.
- The player who passes to the target immediately replaces the target.
- When a ball reaches the target, someone other than the passer of the ball must replace the target.

Four Target Game

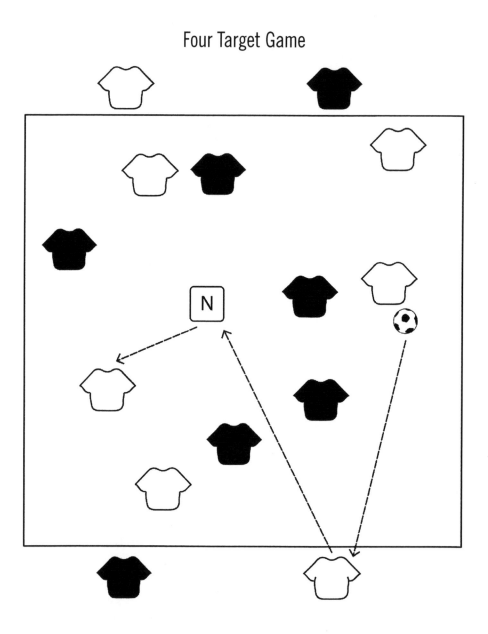

The Endzone Game

Remember when I said this book isn't about penetrating passes? Well I may have lied. This one is for all the readers who are lamenting a lack of drills that turn possession into attacking danger. If my team was stranded on a desert island and I could only bring three drills with me, this would be one of them.

You can set this one up a thousand different ways. You can play with bigger numbers or with two endzones. You can mismatch the teams numerically or play even numbers or even numbers plus a neutral player. You can play pretty much full field if you like. And you can impose all types of restrictions. This drill is more or less a blank canvas limited only by your imagination.

I've found that when introducing the endzone game, it's easiest to start with mismatched numbers until the attackers get the hang of it, so that's what I'm going to diagram for you. We're going to attack 5v3 in a grid that's 25x12. At one end of the grid there is an endzone that is eight yards deep. Because the defending group is down two players, we're going to give them a couple of small counter-attack goals to shoot at just to keep them interested.

For this drill to be successful, you need to pay attention to a few restrictions. The first one is that no player from either team may enter the endzone before the ball; the ball *must* go in first. This is going to be a bigger problem for the defenders than the attackers, because a smart defender's reaction will often be to drop off when a forward pass is about to be played. You've got to keep the defenders from collapsing into their own endzone before the ball enters it, otherwise it's going to be a mess.

The second restriction is that the defenders must maintain some semblance of a shape, and by that I mean they need to have a dedicated midfielder. If the midfielder continuously collapses to form a back-three, the drill is going nowhere.

We're going to start two of the defending players at one end of the grid with their midfielder seven or so yards out in front of them. As for the attacking team, they'll be in a 2-2-1. Their high player will start high up the field and their midfielders will start midway up the field. Their defenders will start on their own end-line.

We start by serving a ball into a defender on the attacking team. At that point, play is live. The objective of the attacking team is to score by connecting a properly timed pass into the endzone and into the run of a teammate. The attacking players may not dribble the ball into the endzone. If the attacking team connects such a pass, they score a point. The defending team scores by shooting into the small counter-attack goals.

Once the players get the hang of it, it's time to add the mother of all restrictions, and this restriction is why I included this drill in a book dedicated to possession. The restriction is that the ball played into the endzone must be a one-touch pass. Believe me, this is going to be a struggle at first, and this is why the attacking team is starting with two extra players.

The final ball restriction means that players have to constantly be thinking about the next ball. The vast majority of the time, to play that final pass, a player must be facing the endzone. That means she is probably receiving the ball from a teammate who is playing with her back to the endzone. So for example, if the target has the ball high up the field and is back-to-pressure, it's not her pass that can play a teammate into the endzone... but the pass she lays back to a teammate can certainly set up that final pass. Teammates have to recognize that the ball back is coming, and therefore a ball forward may be next (*a ball back for a ball forward*), and they have to time their runs accordingly.

To be successful under this restriction, the attacking players have to be thinking two passes ahead and taking care of the details, and that's a lot like possession soccer. And that's why this drill is in this book.

Once your players get the hang of it, and it may take quite a while, advance to bigger numbers and then even numbers and with other touch restrictions. If your team can play this game well at big and even numbers, your opponents are going to have problems.

Bonus Tip: This is an excellent game to emphasize positional interchange and specifically, overlapping runs. If the attackers aren't interchanging positions, they'll struggle to score, particularly under the *final ball* restriction. I've seen this exercise go very stagnant – the attacking team is keeping possession but can't figure out how to penetrate and it just looks like 5v3 keep-away. Then someone will make an overlapping run and all types of things will open up and the whole attack will spring to life.

Endzone Game

Here is the starting shape for the endzone game.

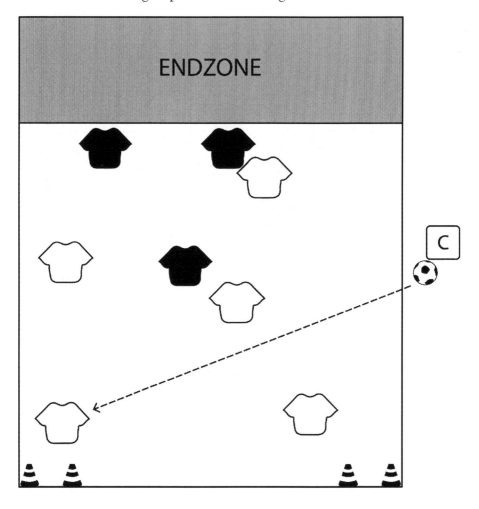

Endzone Game

Here we have a ball back for a one-touch ball forward that plays an attacking teammate into the endzone. In this drill, the negative pass often sets up the penetrating one.

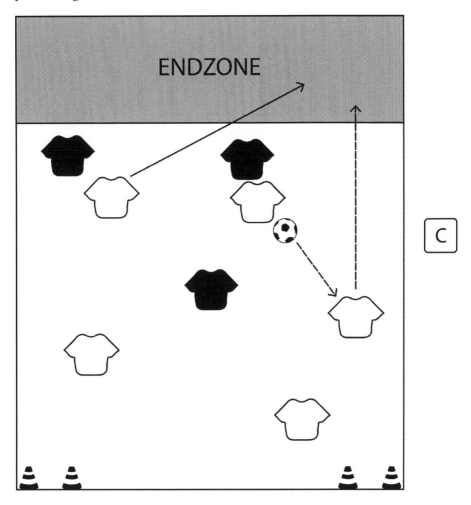

SECTION 6
BIG PICTURE
POSSESSION GAMES

Possession in Systems

I won't diagram the exercises in this section because they're pretty self-explanatory.

Possession in Systems is played between the 18s using the full width of the field and ten players on each team. Each team sets up in a system such as a 4-4-2 or 4-2-3-1. There are no goalkeepers. The offside rule is in effect. There are various ways to score this depending on what your objectives are.

The most basic set up is that a team scores by dribbling across the opponent's end-line or stopping the ball on the opponent's end-line. Another variation is to score it like the endzone game where you have to connect a pass across the opponent's end-line, but the receiver of the pass can't leave the playing area until after the ball has been played.

My favorite scoring system for this drill is to award a point for every one-touch pass a team connects in its attacking half of the field. The pass must originate and be received in the attacking half. I like this variation because it encourages players to keep the ball *and* advance it up the park. Some teams can keep the ball for eons is they go sideways or backwards, but they really struggle to go forward. This gives your team the confidence to keep the ball in the opponent's end of the field.

I also like this scoring system for its incentive to win back the ball in the opponent's end of the field, but that's a discussion for another day.

The Sideline Game

In this game, you're going to play across the field from sideline to sideline. Extend one 18 to each side line. That extended line is now one of your new sidelines. The midfield stripe is the other. You play the whole width of the field.

Divide into two teams of nine or ten players each. You can add a neutral player if you like. The game is all one-touch. The teams score by stopping the ball on the opponent's end-line. When the game begins, each team has a designate end-line to attack and one to defend. As soon as one team scores, they maintain possession of the ball and immediately attack the other end-line. To clarify, whenever someone scores, the teams flop directions. Your players will screw this up and both teams will end up trying to attack the same direction, so make sure they understand the whole flop concept.

The one-touch restriction dictates that this game is all about speed of play. When you play any game with a one-touch restriction, the natural byproduct will be a lot of short passes, and the natural byproduct of short passes is a crowd of both teammates and opponents. Because longer passes are often needed to break pressure and find good numbers, players have to work very hard to give close support to the player receiving that long pass.

There is a high level of difficulty to this game. If your team is playing it well, give yourself a pat on the back!

101

101 is my all-time favorite game, and it's all in the scoring system that we initially introduced in 31. It's a good idea to have a scorekeeper assigned to each team, because there's a lot of math in this one.

In the same space we used for the Sideline Game, we're going to play 9v9 plus a neutral player. This is strictly a possession game. There are no goals to attack and there is no offside. There are no touch restrictions, but teams only score a point each time they successfully connect a one-touch pass. The first team to 101 wins.

To spice up the scoring system, a team is awarded five points for a successful wall pass around an opponent. We also give a five-point bonus for a flighted pass over 25 yards that concludes with a successful one-touch layoff. A team will lose five points if it gives away the restart after the ball has gone out of bounds.

26

Take What They Give You

You can run all the possession exercises in the world, and if you do, your players will certainly become better at keeping the ball. But ultimately, passing the ball and keeping the ball isn't what wins you the game. Scoring one more goal than your opponent – that's what wins the game. That's why you need your players to understand the big picture, and that's why your players need to understand risk management. There's a time to play backwards, a time to play sideways, and there are definitely times to play forward. Typically, the forward pass is going to involve more risk than the other two, but let's face it, if you're going to score, you've got to go forward.

For all my talk about keeping the ball, I believe that a player's first look when receiving the ball (or preferably *before* receiving the ball) should be forward. The forward pass has the most impact on the game. The eternal challenge for coaches is teaching our players that fragile balance and getting them to understand the risk/reward ratio of each ball they intend to play.

If you put technical failures aside, all other things being equal, I believe that there are two critical elements to winning with possession soccer. We've already discussed one of them: It takes more than one of them to take the ball from one of us. The other element is the compass for risk management and that is simply: *Take what they give you.*

Your opponent can't take away everything, but most assuredly, it will always take away something. If an opponent is taking away the ball underneath, then it is susceptible to the ball over the top. If it won't give you the middle of field, it has to give you the flanks. Risk management revolves around recognizing what the opponent is taking away and then finding another option. The challenge is to teach your players to make those calculations and to respond accordingly. Too often a player makes up his mind to play a certain pass but doesn't adjust when the opponent eliminates that as a practical option. In the end he plays that pass anyway and the opponent takes the ball and you're left shouting, "Jimmy, don't force it!"

As you run your possession exercises, you'll see countless, countless instances where a player makes up his mind, forces his pass and loses the ball for his team. Remind your players that they have to be both realistic and flexible with their decision making. Remind them to take what they give you.

The forward pass will be there — just not every time you want it to be there. If the opponent is taking that away, then he is giving you something else. Don't fight the current; just take what they give you.

A FINAL WORD

D id you know that UCLA's legendary basketball coach John Wooden ran the same practice every day? And I don't mean almost every day or every day except the day before a big game; I mean he ran the same practice every day of every season for years on end. The practice that Coach Wooden ran on the first day of preseason was the same practice he ran the day before the national championship game. Can you imagine doing that with your soccer team?

A lot of coaches have a mental rolodex of a zillion different drills to teach possession. I'm not one of them. I don't think drills need to be complex to be effective. I'm a fan of function over form, so I gravitate to the simplest drills that effectively teach the topic. I think that as coaches, we sometimes get so enamored of the presentation that we lose sight of the forest for our trees. Listen, you don't have to reinvent the wheel every time you go to the field. Teaching possession isn't about the drills you run; it's about how you coach them. It's about knowing what you're looking for and then demanding excellence in the details. If you are constantly searching for the next great drill, just remind yourself that John Wooden won 10 national championships in a 12-year span.

When you teach possession, don't settle for anything less than excellence. You've got to burn good habits into the souls of your players. When you're running one of these exercises, a player will do something wrong but things will work out in her favor anyway. Don't accept it! This is where coaching makes a big difference in the long haul. Don't let your players skate past the details. As I often tell my players: *Just because you got away with it, that doesn't make it right.* The details matter. Doing the little things correctly all the time will make a big difference at the most important time.

I've tried to give you the details that I've found to be most important. I hope the message came across clearly. If you feel you've gotten your money's worth from this book, I hope you'll be kind enough to leave me a tip by submitting a five-star review on Amazon. I also hope that what you've gained from this book will help you and your team.

I welcome your feedback. Just shoot an email to coach@soccerpoet.com. And I hope you'll be my Twitter friend! My handle is @SoccerPoet.

If you are interested in bringing me out to run a camp with your team, send me an email at coach@soccerpoet.com. You can also email me if you'd like a bulk order of any of my books at a discounted price.

Thanks to Aaron Usiskin for the amazing cover and all those diagrams! I'd also like to thank my proofreaders Rachael Lehner, Rob Marino and Gary Roberts!

OTHER BOOKS BY DAN BLANK

Everything Your Coach Never Told You Because You're a Girl – This is what your coaches would have said to you if you were a boy, told through the story of a small-college team that won more games than it ever had a right to win. It's a straightforward look at the qualities that define the most competitive females.

Soccer iQ Volume 1 – The Amazon #1 best-seller and an NSCAA Soccer Journal Top 5 Book of the Year. The only book written specifically for soccer players.

Soccer iQ Volume 2 – More simple and effective strategies for becoming a smarter soccer player.

HAPPY FEET – How to Be a Gold Star Soccer Parent (Everything the Coach, the Ref and Your Kid Want You to Know) – The book that coaches want parents to read! If you want to maintain your sanity as a coach, *HAPPY FEET* is the best gift you can give a soccer parent! This book includes free companion videos to explain some of soccer's more mysterious concepts such as the advantage rule, offside, soccer systems and combination play. It also explains the most common errors that well-meaning soccer parents make without even realizing it. Prevent headaches before they start by getting soccer parents to read this book.

In My Tribe – Developing a Culture of Kickass in Female Athletes – The follow-up to Everything Your Coach Never Told You Because You're a Girl, this book details the specific tools employed to feed our competitive beast.

ROOKIE – Surviving Your Freshman Year of College Soccer – The ultimate survival guide for the rising college freshman. If your players are planning to play at the college level, give them a head start. I can't possibly explain how much easier their lives will be if they just read this book. Makes a great Signing Day gift!

Shutout Pizza – Smarter Soccer Defending for Players and Coaches – In 2009 Ole Miss led the SEC in goals-against average. In 2010 the Georgia Bulldogs had the league's best defense. This book was the blueprint for those teams. Written for players and coaches of all levels, *Shutout Pizza* is an easy-to-read and comprehensive collection of defending principles, tips, and exercises. Includes over 50 diagrams.

Chapter 39

Keep The Ball Alive

I believe that addressing and training this concept was a major turning point for us during the 2010 season at Georgia. It made such a profound impact that I plan on addressing it with every team I ever coach.

Territorially we were dominant in nearly every game, but we habitually failed to produce the finishing we needed to win. In the attacking third we lacked patience and we lacked discipline. We would press the opponent for long stretches at a time and everything would be going swimmingly. We'd work down the left side, turn around, switch fields and then try the right side, methodically probing for a worthwhile opening. On the sidelines we could see our opponent wilting from the amount of chasing it was forced to do. We could see the opposing players growing tired in body and spirit. We could see that their shape was coming undone and we knew a good scoring chance was just moments away. Then, inevitably, one of our players would lose her patience and hit a low-percentage, off-balance shot from 30 yards that would result in an easy save or a goal kick and would destroy all the momentum we had been building. Or we would attempt a shot from an impossible angle that would sail wide of the post. In effect, we were donating the ball to our opponent for no other reason than someone decided we had gone too long without shooting. It was a very frustrating stretch for us because we were settling for 0-0 ties against teams that we were categorically destroying in the run of play.

Smart players are realistic. They don't let the opponent off the hook with attempts at goal that will never be dangerous. How many goals have you scored from 35 yards? How many have you scored from 35 yards with your weak foot? How many have you scored from 35 yards with your weak foot when you were off balance? If you don't make a habit of scoring from 35 yards... if you haven't done so in three years... maybe you should consider eliminating that choice from your menu.

You need to understand the damage you do to your team when you take unrealistic shots. You need to understand how it affects the big picture. You can't expect to win if you're continually donating the ball to your opponent when you have her on the ropes. Once you understand that, you will become more discerning in your shot selection.

Another common violation of this rule can be found in unrealistic headers, particularly from crosses. When a serve arrives in your opponent's goal area, it arrives as nothing more than the massive potential to become a goal. Your decision upon receiving that cross determines whether or not that potential will be realized.

Too often, a player who has no realistic chance of putting sufficient power on her header will disregard the odds and try to score anyway. Her shot is an easy grab for the goalkeeper and kills her team's chance to create a legitimate chance.

When you arrive at the back post and that cross has you backpedalling away from the goal, you won't score. If the cross doesn't have much pace and you are 16 yards away from the goal, you won't score. And as much as you scoring a goal would make me very happy, there's a time and a place to go to Plan B. If you don't have a realistic chance to score, don't bother shooting. Don't ruin it for everyone. You're better off keeping the ball alive so a teammate might get that realistic chance. Instead of lobbing a soft header at the goalkeeper or trying to score from an impossible angle, knock the ball down to a teammate or to the top of the six or toward the penalty spot where it can be dangerous.

It's not just headers; it's everything. Regardless of your surface choice, if you're going to take a crack at goal, make sure you have a realistic chance of scoring. It doesn't have to be a no-brainer, automatic easy goal. But by the same token, you shouldn't take a shot that cannot possibly score without the help of divine intervention. Be realistic, patient and disciplined. Otherwise you're donating the ball to your opponent and letting her off the hook.

Note for Coaches: When we addressed this at Georgia, something remarkable happened. Our per-game shot total went down, but our goals-per-shot percentage improved dramatically. Instead of taking 27 shots and not scoring, we were taking 17 shots and scoring three times. We kept the ball in the field of play more, and kept possession of it, which wore down our opponents. Our opponents were taking fewer goal kicks so they weren't getting as much rest. Their goalkeepers were handling the ball less which also took away opportunities to rest. If your team is dominating games but not getting results, this is a topic you may want to evaluate.

ABOUT THE AUTHOR

Dan Blank is the author of the Amazon best-seller, *Soccer iQ*, and has been coaching college soccer for over twenty years. He is the first coach in Southeastern Conference history to lead the conference's best defense in consecutive years at different universities (Ole Miss 2009, Georgia 2010). He has an 'A' License from the USSF and an Advanced National Diploma from the NSCAA. You can buy his books and read his blog at www.soccerpoet.com.

Made in the USA
San Bernardino, CA
10 November 2016